ARTISTS AI

Modernist Archaist
Selected Poems by Osip Mandelstam

With new and selected translations by

Charles Bernstein
Clarence Brown and W. S. Merwin
Bernard Meares
Eugene Ostashevsky
Bob Perelman
Kevin M. F. Platt

Edited and with introductory essay by
Kevin M. F. Platt

WHALE AND STAR

CONTENTS

Osip Mandelstam: Modernist Archaist

Kevin M. F. Platt

Poetry is a plough, turning over time so that its deep layers, its fertile black soil, ends up on the surface. There are periods when mankind, not satisfied with the present day, yearning like a ploughman, craves the virgin soil of time. Revolution in the arts inevitably leads to classicism.[1]

The sea, and Homer—love moves all;
Whom should I listen to? Now Homer is silent,
And the sea, black, clamors in lofty oration
And with a heavy rumble reaches my headboard. (48)[2]

Osip Mandelstam, one of the most significant poets of twentieth-century Russian literature, also embodied more fully than any other its profound paradoxes. He was a Jew born in Poland who became a leading Russian poet; a committed Modernist who was faithful to the great examples and strict forms of the past literary tradition; a rebel who rejected the faith and social values of his well-to-do merchant parents, yearning for a new and different future, who died in the same year as his own father. Most strikingly, Mandelstam, a boy with decidedly revolutionary aspirations, who preserved socialist and left-leaning political sympathies into his maturity, was driven from public life in post-revolutionary society, arrested as an enemy of the people, and hounded to death in the Soviet prison camps. Yet while Mandelstam's poetry bore witness to the impossible convulsions of twentieth-century Russian culture and politics, it was by no means limited or defined by these historical contexts. In an early statement of his creative credo Mandelstam wrote: "for an artist, a worldview is a tool or a means, like a hammer in the hands of a mason, and the only reality is the work of art itself."[3] In just this manner, Mandelstam's poetic reality ultimately transcended and outlasted the revolutionary worldview that gave it birth and that murdered the poet. Nearly seventy years on from his death, Mandelstam is a world-renowned poet; the Soviet Union is dust.

At first glance, it is all too easy to conclude that Mandelstam was an absolute anomaly. Russian cultural life of the early twentieth century appears to us now, a century later, as an explosion of movements pursuing extraordinary modes of experimentation at a time when radical artistic innovation was itself still fresh. The literature, art and music of that era appear fully in step with (and partially explained by) a lived experience of total war, social upheaval and bloody revolution during which all past values were cast aside and trampled to the earth. If we were to select one poet as emblematic of that time and place, it would likely be Vladimir Mayakovsky, one of the signatories of the most notorious Russian Futurist manifesto "A Slap in the Face of Public Taste," which brashly called to "throw Pushkin, Dostoevsky, Tolstoy, etc., etc. overboard from the Steamship of Modernity,"[4] who began the early poem "A Few Words about Myself" with the incendiary line, "I love to watch children dying."[5] This was a time when Russian poetry—along with art, politics, technology and philosophy—cut itself loose from the moorings of past history and set out to discover new forms and subjects suitable for a new age. No wonder, one might conclude, that in this brave new world Mandelstam, a poet of traditional poetic forms and weighty references to Homer, Ovid and Dante, as well as the Russian classics Pushkin, Tiutchev and Batiushkov, was homeless, little appreciated and eventually persecuted and martyred.

In many ways, this conception of Mandelstam, the doomed archaist in a time of innovators, is correct. What could appear further from the spirit of the revolutionary year 1917 than, for instance, one of his few poems of late 1917, "Among the priests and elders, the young Levite…" (57)? At first reading, this is a meditation on Jewish history and the anticipation of the coming of Christ, charged with deeply personal significance for Mandelstam, whose spiritual search had taken him from the faith of his family to an intense, mythically enraptured engagement with Christianity. Undoubtedly, the poet's preoccupation with classical and scriptural myth, his reverence for the poetry of the past and the learned subtlety of his literary experiments (easily mistaken for a sort of snobbish elitism) made him an obvious critical and political target among the brash innovators of the early Soviet literary scene. The members of the Acmeist movement, with which Mandelstam was affiliated from the inception of his career in the last decade before the October Revolution, came in the first decade thereafter to be viewed as representatives of an antediluvian past—as Mayakovsky put it in remarks concerning the other great figure of this movement, Anna Akhmatova, poets of this school were "pointless, pathetic and comic anachronisms."[6] The revolutionary leader Leon Trotsky, reacting perhaps to Mandelstam's abiding interest in Medieval and Renaissance culture, commented in the early 1920s: "Write about whatever you like! But please do permit the new class, that considers, with some justification, that it has been called to create a new world, to point out to you in any case: it does not make new poets of you to translate the *weltanschaung* of a medieval instructional tract into the language of the Acmeists."[7]

However, to conclude with Mayakovsky and Trotsky that Mandelstam was nothing more than an obsolete holdover from a distant epoch is too easy, for it overlooks the complexity of both Mandelstam and of the times in which he lived. To stick with the example of the poem just mentioned, "Among the priests and elders, the young Levite...," in addition to its biographical significance, this short lyric is also, and just as significantly, a projection of biblical history onto the revolutionary era:

He said: the heavens' yellow is disquieting.
Night gathers over the Euphrates—flee, o Hierarchs!
But the elders thought: the guilt is not with us;
Lo, the black-yellow light; lo, the joy of Judea.

Through its "black-yellow light," Mandelstam associates that distant evening in Jerusalem not only with the colors of a Jewish prayer shawl, but also with those of the Imperial Russian flag. In the myth of Jewish premonition and anticipation of the messiah, the poet has encoded the present moment—in which, he hoped, the old world would be reborn into a new and better one that would fully realize the promise of Judeo-Christian history. Mandelstam himself may perhaps be identified in the figure of the young Levite who prophesies the turning of history's wheel in the stanza cited above. Significantly, in the final stanza he abandons the priests of the old religion and gravitates towards a new faith.[8] This double allegory, refracting both personal biography and political history through the prism of ancient myth—biblical here, but just as often it was Greek mythology, or Latin, or all of these at once—is typical for Mandelstam, and remained a standard tool in his poetic repertoire throughout his career. One may note, somewhat tangentially, that Mandelstam was far from alone in viewing the communist revolution through a decidedly religious lens—as the potential culmination of Judeo-Christian moral and spiritual history. Another prominent example of this tendency is presented by the leading poet of the preceding generation, Alexander Blok, whose masterful poem of 1919, "The Twelve," allegorically envisions the revolution as a pack of anarchic soldiers, patrolling the streets of St. Petersburg in a winter storm, pursuing a figure whom they can barely perceive—their unacknowledged leader, Christ himself.

And this gives us a key to unlock Mandelstam's poetry, to comprehend that it, too, constituted a form of modernist innovation. In distinction from radical thinkers like Mayakovsky or Trotsky, who imagined revolution as a total rupture in time, in which an absolutely novel and superior future breaks off from a fallen and corrupt past, Mandelstam understood the revolutionary present as a transcendence of history, in which past epochs had become available in a new way for reinterpretation and reinscription with truer and more vital meaning. For Mandelstam, the past was not a completed era, a dead letter or an unwanted inheritance weighing down later generations, fit only to be "thrown overboard." Rather, the past was an uncharted territory that only could be fully mapped and understood by the revolutionary present. Just as the Old Testament, according to traditional Christian theology, truly made sense when it could be read as the prefiguration of the New, the past was a code to be deciphered, or a nation awaiting redemption, by a Modernist prophet. As he wrote in 1921:

> One often hears: "That's fine and good, but it's yesterday." But I say: Yesterday has not yet been born. In reality, it hasn't even taken place yet. I want Ovid, Pushkin and Catullus all over again—I'm not satisfied with the historical Ovid, Pushkin and Catullus.[9]

Mandelstam's conception of the interdependence of innovation and tradition has been compared with some justification to that of another great traditionalist-Modernist, T. S. Eliot, who famously described innovative poetry as a kind of chemical agent, catalyzing a reconfiguration of the components of the preceding tradition as it created a new place for itself in the history of culture.[10]

Yet Eliot, in the relatively politically stable Anglo-American world, did not sense the grandest implications of this sort of approach to Modernism, which were readily apparent to his Russian contemporary. As Mandelstam goes on to explain in the essay cited above, "The Word and Culture," it is the unique vocation and duty of the poet in a revolutionary era to carry out this reinvention of the past for the good of the nation as a whole. In an age plagued by the dangerous misconception that the past could be discarded entirely, that poetic language itself could be wiped clean or reinvented from scratch, the true poet was called to midwife a rebirth of the sacred myths preserved in past human language:

> This is a heroic age in the life of the word. The word — is flesh and bread. And it shares the fate of bread and flesh: suffering. People are hungry. Hungrier still is the state. But there is something even hungrier: time, that would consume the state itself. [...] Who will raise up the word and show it to time? [...] Compassion for a culture that has renounced the word—this is the social fate and great deed of the contemporary poet.[11]

By this account, even if certain representatives of the state and spokesmen of competing poetic movements viewed him as an anachronistic crank, Mandelstam's poetry was performing the most valuable and heroic function of all for revolutionary society. For only a nation armed with history could chart a course forward through a sea of forgetfulness:

> Well, let's give it a try: a huge, clumsy
> Grinding turn of the wheel.
> The earth sets sail. Take courage, men.
> Dividing the ocean like a plow,
> We will remember even in frigid Lethe
> That this one earth cost us ten heavens. (62)

With regard to the 1920s, a decade of diverse social and cultural experimentation, the comprehension of Mandelstam I have outlined here is sufficient to place the disdain of Mayakovsky and Trotsky into context: these were barbs directed at a competing conception of Modernist poetry and of revolution by the spokesmen of the dominant school of thought. Yet if we turn to consider the 1930s, when Stalin consolidated absolute power and constructed a totalitarian society, it becomes plain why Mandelstam's vision of time and culture presented more than just competition for the regnant views, but rather a superior and threatening critique of them.

It is by now well established (by history itself, one might say) that the Bolsheviks were poor Marxists. Among their oversights were the many lucid warnings of Marx himself that the revolutionary transformation of human society by political will and decree is a tricky undertaking—that those who attempt forcibly to forget the past are in danger of repeating it: "the tradition of all the dead generations weighs like a nightmare on the brain of the living."[12] By the early 1930s, the Soviet Union had come to exemplify perfectly the ironic tendency of revolutions to wind up as rehearsals of past history, intentionally or otherwise. Under Stalin, time's contrary undercurrents played out in a particularly horrific manner, as this "most progressive state in history" came to institute the most antiquated and abusive political principles imaginable in new and frightening forms—from despotic systems of coercion and social control to rigidly imposed orthodox beliefs. Of course, the most important tenet of the Soviet "state religion" remained the absolute novelty of revolutionary society—this was an article of faith that was defended with violence that grew in proportion to its patent inaccuracy. In this light, Mandelstam's base conception of the necessary interconnection of a revolutionary present with an ever-present, fluid and reinvented past came to seem both prophetic and criminally threatening. Ultimately, persecution of this poet should not be taken simply as the elimination by radical innovators of their "natural" opponent, the archaist. Instead, this was the eradication of a critic who was uniquely equipped to unmask the absurdity of the official conception of revolutionary innovation—by offering in its place a more coherent version than the representatives of the state could themselves imagine. This is not to say that the poet was sent to the camps for these specific, almost metaphysical reasons, but that his death is a comprehensible outcome of the political reality of his times, which were to a remarkable extent governed by metaphysical commitments.

In truth, Mandelstam's comprehension of history was simply more workable, more realistic, than that of his oppressors, who remained stubbornly blind to the echoes of the past in the Soviet present. Mandelstam sensed from the start of his career that radical transformation is always unavoidably also a reinvention of the past. One of the greatest ironies of this situation is that this doomed, unorthodox poet, in his efforts to make a place for himself in Soviet society, composed what are perhaps the most sublime lines ever dedicated to Stalin himself. Who better than Mandelstam, the Modernist steeped in the poetry of classical Roman antiquity, to find the proper mode of poetic address for this paradoxically most modern and most archaic dictator:

> If I took up charcoal to offer highest praise
> In a drawing of incontestable joy,
> I'd sketch the air in cunning angles,
> Both carefully and anxiously.
> So that the present would resound in the features
> With an artistry bordering on insolence,
> I'd tell of him who moved earth's axis, with reverence
> For the custom of a hundred and forty nations.
> I'd raise the slightest corner of one brow,
> And raise it yet again in different resolution;
> Pay heed: Prometheus has blown his coal alight!
> Attend, Aeschylus: as I draw, I weep! (137)

Ultimately, this "Poem About Stalin," along with the rest of Mandelstam's works, achieved a place in history that outshines that of the despot it glorified. Yet in its more mundane purpose it was a failure. A desperate stab at remedying a bad situation—an attempt which the poet later explained to Akhmatova as "an illness"—this grandiloquent poem could not halt the process of persecution that had begun in 1934 with a very different poem about the Soviet leader—a work that tragically proved to be, for his own biography, yet another of Mandelstam's prophetic works:

He forges decree after decree like horseshoes—
Hitting one in the groin; another in temple, brow, or eye. (118)

•

Osip Emilevich Mandelstam was born in Warsaw, Poland (then a part of the Russian Empire) on January 3, 1891. It is not known how long his family resided in that city, in particular, but his parents were certainly representative of the complexity of Jewish life around the turn of the century in what is now largely Eastern Europe. His mother, Flora Osipovna Mandelstam (neé Verblovskaia; cir. 1866–1916), was a member of the educated Jewish bourgeoisie of the prosperous Baltic city of Vilnius, who had received a solid musical training in her girlhood and spoke in a bookish, proper Russian. His father, Emil (cir. 1851–1938), was a leather craftsman who by dint of his industriousness in developing his workshop rose in wealth and social standing to the point that he could relocate his family in 1894 to Pavlovsk, an elite and fashionable suburb of St. Petersburg, the capital of the Empire. (At the time, only Jews of considerable economic or social weight could receive permission to reside in central Russian cities.) As one gleans from Mandelstam's autobiography, "The Noise of Time" (1923), the poet later self-consciously dismissed the provinciality and lack of cultural definition of his childhood family as "Judaic chaos."[13] Yet for all that, in his parents' social and cultural mobility, in their aspiration to modern forms of success and to cosmopolitan cultural life— hallmark features of the urban European Jewry of this era— one may sense the spiritual foundations of the future poet, who carried these aspirations to a logical outcome by becoming a self-made citizen of secular European culture at large.

Around 1897 the family, which grew to include three boys, moved into St. Petersburg itself, where Emil Mandelstam's business prospered for the next decade or so. In the uncertain economic and social circumstances following the 1905 revolution in Russia, however, his fortunes reversed, driving him to near bankruptcy by the eve of the revolutions of 1917. The move to the imperial capital, which the poet would still identify as "my city, familiar as tears" (99) in the 1930s, after a long absence, in many ways determined Mandelstam's fate. As Joseph Brodsky wrote:

> If his poetry was sometimes called "Petersburgian," there is more than one reason to consider this definition both accurate and complementary. Accurate because, apart from being the administrative capital of the empire, Petersburg was also the spiritual center of it, and in the beginning of the century the streams of that current were merging there the way they do in Mandelstam's poems. Complementary because both the poet and the city profited in meaning by their confrontation. If the West was Athens, Petersburg, in the teens of this century, was Alexandria. This "window on Europe," as Petersburg was called by Voltaire, this "most invented city," as it was defined later by Dostoevsky [...] was and is beautiful with that kind of beauty which happens to be caused by madness—or which tries to conceal this madness.[14]

In the 1930s, Mandelstam defined the only poetic movement he ever ascribed to, Acmeism, as "a longing for world culture."[15] In light of Brodsky's remarks, it becomes clear that this definition applies equally to the provincial Jew's entry into the universe of Russian and world literature, and to St. Petersburg itself, Russia's foothold in European civilization. The city and the poet were well suited to each other precisely because they each represented an attempt to conjure "world culture" in a place where none had previously been.

In 1899, after a customary elementary instruction at home in basic skills, European languages (French and German) and piano, Mandelstam left his tutors and governesses to finish his education with the children of high society in the progressive Tenishev Commercial Academy. His passions during his school years were divided between revolutionary sympathies—he gravitated towards the anarchist party of the Socialist Revolutionaries—and poetry, which he imbibed from his teacher of literature, the decadent poet Vladimir V. Gippius. By the time he graduated from the Tenishev Academy in 1907, however, he had turned all of his attention to literature. In the subsequent several years he intermittently traveled in Europe, visiting and studying for short periods in France, Italy, Greece and Germany. In Russia he was admitted in 1911 to the St. Petersburg University (after nominally converting to Methodism in Finland in order to get around Jewish enrollment quotas), but only attended sporadically and never completed a degree.

He received his most significant education during these years in St. Petersburg's vibrant, bohemian intellectual and cultural scene, in effete salons and literary cabarets like the famous Stray Dog Café, where poets and critics read avant-garde works and manifestos to an often rowdy public. His first literary mentor was one of the finest and most famous poets of the preceding generation, Viacheslav Ivanov, a leading light of the Symbolist movement then at the height of popularity and influence. As elsewhere in Europe, Symbolism and the related tendency of Decadence were Russia's first Modernist poetic schools. Although Symbolism comprised too broad a grouping of writers to describe adequately in a few words, it has been characterized (to be precise: caricatured) as taking poetry to be a form of mystic delirium or theurgy. For writers like Ivanov, poetry granted access to otherworldly, spiritual and magical realities.

Mandelstam's first serious poems, dating from 1908-09 and printed in his debut publication in 1910, are themselves mildly Symbolist in tone and content. Yet soon enough a group of young poets including Mandelstam broke with their older teachers, setting up their own "Guild of Poets" and proclaiming their new school of poetry. The most notable members of the Guild, apart from Mandelstam, were Nikolai Gumilev and Anna Akhmatova. In opposition to their predecessors' hazy, hand-waving ecstasies, they proclaimed a poetry of concrete images and precise explorations of this world, calling their school of writing "Acmeism" to denote their focus on the fundamental origins of language, sense and experience, as well as their aspirations for a gem-like perfection of form—an acme in poetic craft.

Mandelstam's own manifesto of this period, "The Morning of Acmeism," described the group's mission with an extended metaphor of architecture and masonry:

> The blade of Acmeism is not the stiletto or the sting of Decadence. Acmeism is for those who, possessed by the spirit of building, do not timorously reject their own weight, but rather joyfully accept it in order to awaken and make use of the forces sleeping within for the purposes of architecture. [...] It's as though the stone grew hungry for a different mode of existence and discovered the dynamic potential hidden within itself—as though it asked to be taken up into the vaulted ceiling—in order to participate in a joyful equilibrium with others like itself. [...] We cannot fly. We can only climb the towers that we ourselves construct.[16]

In keeping with these conceptions, Mandelstam's first collection was titled *Stone* (1913; expanded ed., 1914), and included programmatic works reflecting the Acmeist agenda (his stunning architectural poems "Hagia-Sophia" [42] and "Notre Dame" [41]) and a pronounced overall emphasis on precise language and concrete subject matter. Yet it should be said that Acmeist "doctrine" was never much of a constraint on practice—each member of the group (which at five poets can hardly be called a movement) forged an individual path. The Acmeist moment was short-lived, and would have been a blip in the history of Russian poetry if not for its significance as a launching-pad for Akhmatova and Mandelstam, both of whom built the defining impetus of their poetry on Acmeist foundations. In retrospect, however, it might be more just to reverse the formula—to conclude that Acmeism only gained definition and historical gravity from the writing of these two, who would continue their alliance to the end, never affiliating themselves with any other "-ism," no matter how modish or politically orthodox.

During the years of WWI and up to the 1917 revolutions, Mandelstam led the life of a professional poet, with little money, few belongings and no fixed place of residence. In his migrations between the Crimea and Petrograd (as St. Petersburg was renamed in a demonstration of anti-German sentiment), he became acquainted with and enamored of Marina Tsvetaeva, a young poet whose avant-garde brilliance matched his own. Although he experienced a bout of patriotic identification with the Russian cause, Mandelstam quickly came, with Russian society as a whole, to descry the folly and slaughter of the war. He was witness to the February and the October revolutions in 1917, and though his sympathies lay with the Socialist Revolutionaries rather than the Bolsheviks, he made his peace with the latter's grip on power soon enough. During the next few years, when the country was divided and wracked by civil war, the poet continued his unsettled movements across the landscape. He seems to have been under the protection of some minor deity of literature: twice arrested by different warring sides in the Crimea and then in Georgia, he was both times released because someone knew him by reputation and admired his poetry. In Ukraine, where he worked for the Soviet powers as a writer and journalist, he met Nadezhda Iakovlevna Khazina, who would soon be his wife and who was fated to become the living repository, by dint of memorization, of much of Mandelstam's later poetry. Her two volumes of masterfully written memoirs contain a wealth of information not only about hers and her husband's lives, but also about Russian culture of the early Soviet period as a whole.

The poetic output of these years, bearing the imprint of war, social upheaval, the poet's relationships with Tsvetaeva and others, as well as the Brownian motion of his biography, was published in 1923 in his second major volume, *Tristia*. In this collection, one witnesses the maturation of Mandelstam's poetic system. Retaining the finely honed laconism of image and language of his earlier work, the poems of *Tristia* develop an extraordinary web of citation and reference, more or less concealed, to mythic archetypes, to the works of Ancient, Russian and European classics and to the poetry of contemporaries. Mandelstam's verse has been described as a "poetry of poetry"—a lacework of borrowed words and lines, artfully joined into a new synthetic whole in which the poet creates a "conversation" of many voices across time and space. This interweaving of elements drawn from the poetic tradition is the technique by which Mandelstam made good on his conception of Modernism as a transcendence of cultural history (discussed above), which he articulated in his critical articles of the early twenties. To be sure, in reading these poems, especially in translation, it is well nigh impossible to catch all of their baggage of interlaced references—and it should be said that one may comprehend their beauty independently of such matters. Nevertheless, an ear tuned to the echoes of alien words is perhaps the most crucial skill a reader can bring to Mandelstam.

One should not imagine that the poet, grown up and married, now settled down in domestic bliss. Instead, Nadezhda

Mandelstam took up her husband's uncertain mode of life. They were marvelously unpractical people who lived by and for literature and paid little attention to mundane questions of clothing, food and money. Often reduced to living on handouts from more successful or more conventional friends, to the end of their years together they had little by way of possessions and remained in nearly constant motion from place to place, apartment to apartment, city to city. While Mandelstam at times was employed as a journalist or had a more or less regular gig as a translator, his work relationships were also invariably short-lived. In the twenties, at least, these conditions were the result of the poet's choice and temperament. In general, the Soviet Union's Bolshevik rulers adopted a *laissez faire* attitude towards cultural life during their first decade in power, which allowed a feverish, contentious, wild flowering of art and literature. Mandelstam's run-ins with critical opponents and his legal entanglements (although innocent of the charge, he was sued for plagiarism in connection with a translation in the late 1920s) were neither unusual nor unusually threatening during these years. Although the poet did not enjoy anything like solid official patronage, he had the support of the editor of an influential literary journal and, more importantly, of a powerful member of the Bolshevik Central Committee, Nikolai Bukharin. Helped by such connections, Mandelstam published a volume of criticism and a retrospective of his poetry in state publishing houses in 1928. This would be the last collection of his poetry published in his lifetime.

In the late twenties Mandelstam gave up poetry for a period of five years, turning his energies entirely to short prose fiction and critical writing. No full explanation for this switch has been reconstructed, but the sparse record of his last poems before this hiatus indicates that perhaps the task that the poet had set himself, of joining the culture of the past to that of the new Soviet world, had begun to seem beyond his powers:

My age, my animal, who will ever be able
To glance into your pupils
And cement together with his blood
The vertebrae of two centuries? (83)

The impetus for a return to poetry came in 1930 on a state-sponsored trip to Armenia arranged by Bukharin. Besides eliciting the extraordinary travelogue "Journey to Armenia," this hiatus in a land that Mandelstam experienced as one of the ancient sites of Hellenic Christian culture jolted him once again into poetic voice. Yet Mandelstam returned to a very different literary scene. By the late 1920s, Stalin had embarked on his vicious program of consolidating absolute power, while the government apparatus beneath him had begun the equally vicious process of creating a state-controlled society in which not only the economy but newspapers, fashion and consumer taste, children's literature and fine art were all governed by official directives. Paradoxically, in this increasingly oppressive social and political climate Mandelstam seems to have gathered new confidence in his chosen role as champion of cultural continuity. As the late scholar M. L. Gasparov explained, official Soviet culture had declared itself the sole heir of world culture. Yet when it proved to be unworthy of that inheritance, in the poet's eyes, Mandelstam was enabled once more defiantly to stake his own claim.[17] His return to poetry brought a third period, or perhaps a third layer of complexity, to his poetic craft, which now expanded its range of vocabulary towards jargon and street language and which became almost telegraphic in its compression and density. The thirties, in terms of the sheer quantity of poems written, became the most productive period of the poet's career. Yet all of the poetic outpouring of this period was captured in notebooks and manuscripts that were only preserved through the determination and courage of Nadezhda Mandelstam and others, to be published decades later in a future that must have seemed a barely tenable hope at the time.

This last decade of the poet's life took place almost entirely under the shadow of his impending death, which he himself anticipated as an inevitable result of his uncompromising stance towards the demands of Soviet society—Akhmatova recalled him telling her that he was "prepared for death" in 1934.[18] In these years, wandering and homelessness resulted not from personal choice, but from the repressive measures of the literary and police establishment. From the early 1930s, he was subjected to hostile criticism in the press, and as a result was unable to publish much or support himself. Mandelstam's epigram on Stalin, recited to a small circle of listeners, constituted a straightforward challenge to the state, and has been viewed by some as a consciously suicidal act. It was a deliberately composed insult of a remarkably personal, almost childishly taunting nature:

> His meaty fingers are fat as worms,
> And his words are solid as ten-pound weights. (120)

Betrayed by an informant, Mandelstam was arrested in May, 1934. Remarkably, as a result of the intercessions of Bukharin and the poet Boris Pasternak, he was sentenced only to exile, first in a remote town in the Urals, Cherdyn. There, he was afflicted by a psychotic attack and attempted to kill himself by throwing himself from a window. His and his wife's appeals, pleading his ill health, resulted in his exile being relocated to the relatively cosmopolitan central Russian city of Voronezh. Stalin is supposed to have ruled personally that the poet should be "isolated, but preserved."[19] During the following years, Mandelstam's poetic productivity increased in seeming proportion to his desperation and sense of persecution, resulting in the rich and moving works of the Voronezh notebooks. This was the final stage of his career, as he appears to have known well. Following the end of his term of exile, in 1937, he and Nadezhda returned once again to live near Moscow, although as a convict he was not permitted to reside in the capital itself. This was the height of the mass arrests, shootings, show trials and prison camps of Stalin's Great Terror. In May, 1938 the poet was arrested again and sentenced to five years in the camps "for counterrevolutionary activity." Exhausted and sick, Mandelstam died in a prison clinic in Siberia on December 27, 1938.

Suggestions for Further Reading

Other editions of Mandelstam's work in English:

Osip Mandelstam. *50 Poems*. Bernard Meares, trans. New York: Persea Books, 1977.

Osip Mandelstam. *The Moscow Notebooks*. Richard and Elizabeth McKane, trans. Newcastle upon Tyne: Bloodaxe Books, 1991.

Osip Mandelstam. *The Prose of Osip Mandelstam*. Clarence Brown, ed. and trans. Oxford: Oxford University Press, 1966.

Osip Mandelstam. *Selected Poems*. Clarence Brown and W. S. Merwin, trans. New York: Atheneum, 1974.

Osip Mandelstam. *Selected Poems*. David McDuff, trans. New York: Farrar, Straus and Giroux, 1975.

Memoirs and biography:

Clarence Brown. *Mandelstam*. Cambridge: Cambridge University Press, 1973.

Nadezhda Mandelstam. *Hope Against Hope*. New York: Atheneum, 1978.

Nadezhda Mandelstam. *Hope Abandoned*. New York: Atheneum, 1974.

Scholarly studies of Mandelstam:

Clare Cavanagh. *Osip Mandelstam and the Modernist Creation of Tradition*. Princeton: Princeton University Press, 1995.

Gregory Freidin. *A Coat of Many Colors: Osip Mandelstam and His Mythologies of Self-Presentation*. Berkeley: University of California Press, 1987.

Omry Ronen. *An Approach to Mandelstam*. Jerusalem: The Magnes Press, 1983.

Kiril Taranovsky. *Essays on Mandelstam*. Cambridge: Harvard University Press, 1976.

Osip Mandelstam. *Selected Poems*. James Greene, trans. London: Penguin Books, 1991.

Note on Translation, Selection of Poems, Transliteration and Acknowledgments

The poems offered in this volume present an overview of Mandelstam's major works. For the first three divisions of the volume I have adopted the titles of the poet's published books, although I have taken the liberty of including some poems from the corresponding years that were not printed in those collections. This volume draws on two previous translation efforts: by Bernard Meares and by the team comprised of Clarence Brown and W. S. Merwin.[20] About half the poems published below are new renderings of Mandelstam's poetry into English: some by the poet and scholar Eugene Ostashevsky; some by myself in collaboration with either Charles Bernstein or with Bob Perelman; and some by myself alone. All of these new translations are based on the most recent authoritative Russian edition of Mandelstam's works.[21] In some cases, the decision to offer a new translation was motivated by a desire to present English readers with a different or more precise version of an important poem. In others, new translations are based on fuller knowledge of the final versions of Mandelstam's works than was available to earlier translators. (NB: because of the difficult circumstances for scholarship presented by a repressed poet such as Mandelstam, many of whose works remained unpublished until long after his death, a fully informed reconstruction of the final versions of many poems only became possible in the post-Soviet era.) My only editorial intervention into previously published translations has been to correct dates of composition according to the most recent scholarly consensus. Russian names are printed in this edition in their accepted English versions (Mandelstam), with the exception of bibliographical entries for Russian language publications, where I have used the standard Library of Congress transliteration system (Mandel'shtam).

Readers of this collection will notice clear distinctions between the linguistic and formal properties of the poems that follow, reflecting several very distinct approaches to translation included here. Bernard Meares undertook in his translations to approximate the metrical structure and often even the rhyme scheme of the originals, and in general rendered Mandelstam into a formal, restrained English that captures something of the Russian poet's sometimes very erudite and literary language. In contrast, Clarence Brown and W. S. Merwin transported Mandelstam's voice into the *vers libre* and sophisticated, yet not bookish, idiom that is characteristic of post-WWII American poetry of which Merwin is a leading representative.[22] Ostashevsky's translations present a rendering of Mandelstam into a more contemporary poetic voice, one that often evokes in its daring something of the Modernist innovation of Mandelstam's language. My collaborative efforts with Bernstein and Perelman have striven for a sparse, sculptural style that communicates other features of the original "masonry" of Mandelstam's works. The versions I have created working alone strive to give a more precise rendering of the sense and order of elements of the original, often slightly deforming the English in order to "trace over" the Russian—in so doing signaling the foreignness of Mandelstam's poetry. Although some readers may find the resulting polyphony of the collection as a whole jarring at times, my hope is that it will allow readers without knowledge of Russian a more complete comprehension of Mandelstam by means of a textual "triangulation" on his voice. Perfect translation of poetry is, of course, an impossible goal, yet many different approximations of a distant original, laying one on top of another, may render a sharper outline in aggregate than any one rendering can in isolation.

Finally, I offer grateful acknowledgement to Bernard Meares, Clarence Brown and W. S. Merwin for allowing the inclusion of their previously published translations. Thanks go to Eugene Ostashevsky for his renderings of Mandelstam. Charles Bernstein and Bob Perelman have generously contributed time, thought and energy to our joint translations and have critiqued my solo translations. For additional reivew of my own translations and suggestions for improvement, my gratitude goes to Bernard Meares, Karina Sotnik and Timothy Sergay. Finally, many thanks are due to Enrique Martínez Celaya for proposing this project and making it possible through the support of his publishing house Whale and Star, as well as to Jillian Taylor at Whale and Star for administrative support and production of the volume.

1908 – 1915
Stone

All the lamps were turned low.
You slipped out quickly in a thin shawl.
We disturbed no one.
The servants went on sleeping.

1908

I've been given a body. What should I do with it,
So singular, so my own?

For this joy, quiet, to live and breathe,
Who, tell me, am I to thank?

I am gardener, but flower too;
In the world's dungeon I am not alone.

On the windowpanes of eternity,
My breath, my warmth has already settled.

On it a pattern is pressed,
Unrecognizable of late.

Even if moment's gloom streams down—
The pattern, so dear, won't be crossed out!

1909

SILENTIUM

It has not yet been born;
It is both music and word,
And therefore, of all that lives
It is the indestructible bond.

The sea's breast calmly breathes,
But the day, insane, is bright;
Pale lilac of froth
In a black-azure vessel.

Oh let my lips attain
Primordial silence,
Like a crystalline tone,
Pure from birth!

Aphrodite, remain as foam;
And, word, return into music;
Shun others' hearts, o heart,
United with life's origin!

1910

THE LUTHERAN

As I was out walking I met a funeral,
last Sunday, by the Lutheran church,
and I stayed idly attending
the stern grief of the faithful.

None of the words of their language came through.
Nothing gleamed but the thin bridles
and the dull glint of the horseshoes, reflected
on the street empty for Sunday.

But in the rocking dusk of the hearse
where the dummy sadness had retired
the autumn roses lay in their buttonhole
without a word or a tear.

Foreigners in black ribbons came walking behind
beside the women weak with weeping,
veils drawn across red faces.
The implacable coachman kept moving on.

Whoever you were, vanished Lutheran
don't worry, it went off well.
The proper tears dimmed the proper eyes,
the right bells rang through the autumn.

And I thought plain thoughts, as was fitting.
We're not prophets nor apostles.
Hell has no fears for us, we repent for no heaven.
Our candles make a twilight at noon.

1912

NOTRE DAME

Where the Roman justice judged a foreign people,
Stands the basilica; first and joyous,
Just like Adam, with nerves stretching,
The vault, a cross of air, flexes its muscles.

But outside a secret plan emerges:
Here labored the strength of arching stone
So the freighted mass won't crush the walls,
And the cocky vault's battering ram is still.

Elemental labyrinth, inscrutable forest,
The gothic soul's rationalized abyss,
Egyptian awe and Christian timidity,
Reed by oak and plumb-line's king of all.

But, citadel of Notre Dame, the closer
I studied your preternatural ribs,
The more I thought: from crude weight
Someday I too will fashion the beautiful.

1912

HAGIA SOPHIA

Hagia Sophia—Lord decreed
Nations and kings shall stop here!
Truly your cupola hangs, in the words of a witness,
As if by a chain from the heavens.

And for the ages, Justinian's example:
When Diana of Ephesus allowed
One hundred and seven green marble pillars
To be plundered for foreign gods.

But what was your generous maker thinking,
When, in soul and concept high,
He arranged apses and exedrae,
Directing them West and East?

Beautiful temple, bathed in the world,
And forty windows—a triumph of light;
On the spandrels, beneath the cupola, four
Archangels—most beautiful of all.

And the wise, spherical building
Will outlast nations and ages,
And the seraphims' resonant sobs
Won't warp dark gilt.

1912

PETERSBURG STANZAS

to N. Gumilev

Above the yellow of government buildings
A dull blizzard whirled at length,
And once again a jurist settles into a sleigh,
Sweeping shut, with a flourish, his overcoat.

Steamships are holed up for the winter. The sun's heat
Has scorched the thick glass of the cabin window.
Monstrous, like a battleship in dock,
Russia is heavily at rest.

But on the Neva stand the embassies of half the world,
The Admiralty, sunshine, calm!
And the state's severe purple
Is as coarse and poor as a hair shirt.

Heavy is the burden of a northern snob—
Onegin's ancient melancholy;
On the Senate Square: snowdrift's bank,
Fire's smoke and bayonet's cold.

Yawls chopped at waves, and seagulls
Called on the hemp storehouse,
Where, selling honey-ale and rolls,
Only operatic peasants stroll.

A winding line of autos flies through the mist;
A shy, self-centered pedestrian—
The crank Evgeny—ashamed of his poverty,
Breathes in exhaust and curses fate![23]

1913

THE ADMIRALTY

In the northern capital a dusty poplar languishes.
The translucent clockface is lost in the leaves,
and through the dark green a frigate or acropolis
gleams far away, brother of water and sky.

An aerial ship and a touch-me-not mast,
a yardstick for Peter's successors, teaching
that beauty is no demigod's whim
it's the plain carpenter's fierce rule-of-eye.

The four sovereign elements smile on us,
but man in his freedom has made a fifth.
Do not the chaste lines of this ark
deny the dominion of space?

The capricious jellyfish clutch in anger,
anchors are rusting like abandoned ploughs—
and behold the locks of the three dimensions are sprung
and all the seas of the world lie open.[24]

1913

Poison in the bread, the air drunk dry.
Hard to doctor the wounds.
Joseph sold into Egypt
grieved no more bitterly for home.

Bedouins under the stars
close their eyes, sitting their horses,
and improvise songs
out of the troubles of the day.

No lack of subject:
one lost a quiver in the sand,
one bartered away a stallion...
the mist of events drifts away.

And if the song is sung truly,
from the whole heart, everything
at last vanishes: nothing is left
but space, the stars, the singer.

1913

AKHMATOVA

Pausing in a half turn—o, sorrow!—
She glanced at the indifferent crowd.
Falling from her shoulder, her stole,
Faux-classical, became as stone.

Ominous voice—bitter, heady herb—
Unfetters the soul's depths:
Thus, as an indignant *Phèdre*,
Once stood Rachelle.[25]

1914

There are orioles in the woods, and vowel length
Is the one measure of tonic verse.
But only once per year does duration spill out
In nature as it does in Homer's meters.

The day is sundered as though by a caesura;
Calm since morning, with difficult expanses;
Oxen are at pasture; too great a golden languor
To draw a whole note's riches from the reed.

1914

Insomnia. Homer. Taut sails.
I've read the catalogue of ships halfway:
This drawn-out brood, this string of cranes,
That once rose above Hellas.

As a wedge of cranes flies to alien lands—
Divine foam on kings' heads—
Where do you sail to? If not for Elena,
What could Troy alone hold for you, Achaeans?

The sea, and Homer—love moves all.
Whom should I listen to? Now Homer is silent,
And the sea, black, clamors in lofty oration
And with a heavy rumble reaches my headboard.

1915

1916 – 1920
Tristia

to Marina Tsvetaeva

On a sled covered with straw.
Our own matting scarcely covered us.
We rode through wide Moscow
from the Sparrow Hills to a little church we knew well.

Children in Uglich play at knucklebones.
A smell of bread baking.
I am taken through streets bareheaded.
In the chapel three lighted candles.

Not three lights but three meetings,
one blessed by God himself.
There will be no fourth. Rome is far.
And He never loved it.

The sled drove along black ruts.
People coming back from their walks.
Thin *muzhiks* and cross old women
restless at the gate.

In the raw distance a night of birds rose.
The bound hands went numb.
They're bringing the Tsarevich. The body turns to ice.
They set fire to the straw.[26]

1916

In transparent Petropolis we will die.
Where Persephone reigns over us.
We drink in mortal vapors at each sigh,
And for us each hour is a year of death.

Sea goddess, fearsome Athena,
Remove your mighty stone helmet.
In transparent Petropolis we will die.
Not you, but Persephone reigns here.[27]

1916

This night is beyond repair,
But for you it is still light!
At the gates of Jerusalem
A black sun has risen.

The yellow sun is more frightful—
Rock-a-bye, hush my child—
In the bright temple, the Jews
Have buried my mother.

Lacking grace,
Deprived of sanctity,
In the bright temple, the Jews
Have sung a wife's ashes to rest.

And over my mother rang
The voices of Israelites.
I awoke in a cradle
Illuminated by a black sun.[28]

1916

SOLOMINKA

I

Solominka, when you can't sleep in the huge chamber,
when you lie awake under the steep ceiling
waiting for its indifference to descend
onto your eyelids that feel everything,

dry Solominka, little ringing straw
who sipped up the whole of death—it has made you gentle.
The little dead straw has broken. It was Solominka.
No, not Salomea. It was the dead one.

Sleep won't come, but things grow heavier.
There are less of them than there were. And what silence!
The pillows hardly show in the mirror.
The bed floats on a lake, on a glass.

But that's not Solominka, under the grave satin,
above the black Neva, in the huge chamber.
The twelve months are singing of the hour of death
and the blue air is a river pale with ice.

The breath of grave December is flowing.
The room fills with the whole weight of the Neva.
It's not Solominka, it's Ligeia, dying.
I have learned you, blessed words.

II

I have learned you, blessed words.
Lenore, Solominka, Ligeia, Seraphita.
The huge room is full of the whole weight of the Neva.
Blood runs pale-blue from the granite.

Grave December gleams above the Neva.
The twelve months sing of the hour of death.
No, that's not Solominka, under the grave satin,
the dry straw sipping the deadly peace.

In my blood Ligeia is December.
Her blessed voice is asleep in the lidded stone.
But pity killed Solominka—or Salomea.
Whichever it was will never return.[29]

1916

The thread of gold cordial flowed from the bottle
with such languor that the hostess found time to say
here in mournful Tauris where our fates have cast us
we are never bored—with a glance over her shoulder.

On all hands the rites of Bacchus, as though the whole world
held only guards and dogs. As you go you see no one.
And the placid days roll past like heavy barrels. Far off
in the ancient rooms there are voices. Can't make them out.
  Can't answer.

After tea we went out into the great brown garden.
Dark blinds are dropped like eyelashes on the windows.
We move along the white columns looking at grapes. Beyond them
airy glass has been poured over the drowsing mountains.

I said the grape vines live on like an antique battle,
with gnarled cavalry tangling in curving waves.
Here in stone-starred Tauris is an art of Hellas: here, rusted,
are the noble ranks of the golden acres.

Meanwhile silence stands in the white room like a spinning wheel,
smelling of vinegar, paint, wine cool from the cellar.
Do you remember in the Greek house the wife they all loved?
Not Helen. The other. And how long she embroidered?

Golden fleece, where are you then, golden fleece?
All the way the heaved weight of the sea rumbled.
Leaving his boat and its sea-wearied sails,
Odysseus returned, filled with space and time.

1917

to A. V. Kartashev

Among the priests, the young Levite
Remained long on the morning watch.
The Judaic night grew thick above him;
The ruined temple was rising, sullenly, again.

He said: the heavens' yellow is disquieting.
Night gathers over the Euphrates—flee, o Hierarchs!
But the elders thought: the guilt is not with us;
Lo, the black-yellow light; lo, the joy of Judea.

He was with us when, on the banks of a stream,
We swaddled the Sabbath in priceless linen
And illuminated with a menorah
The Jerusalem night and fumes of nonbeing.[30]

1917

Far away is the gray
transparent spring of asphodels.
For the moment the sand still rustles,
in fact, the wave still seethes.
But here, like Persephone, my soul
enters the fortunate circle.
Such beautiful sunburnt hands as these
are not found in the kingdom of Hades.

Why do we entrust to a boat
the weight of the funeral urn,
and perform the black rose rite
over the amethyst water?
To the sea past Cape Meganom,
through the fogs, my soul is fighting;
a black sail will come back from there
after the burial.

How fast the unlighted bank
of storm clouds passes,
and under this windy moon
black rose petals are flying.
And that bird of death and grief,
the huge flag, memory,
trails from the cypress stern
a black border.

The sad fan of the past
opens with a hiss, toward the place
where the amulet was buried,
with a dark shudder, in the sand.
To the sea past Cape Meganom,
through the fogs, my soul is fighting;
a black sail will come back from there
after the burial.

1917

TO CASSANDRA

I did not seek in those budding moments
Your lips, Cassandra, your eyes, Cassandra,
But in December—a solemn wakefulness—
Remembrance torments us!

And in December of 1917
We lost everything, loving:
One is robbed by the people's will,
Another has robbed himself...

Some day in that foolish capital,
At a Scythian festival, on the Neva's banks,
To the sounds of a loathsome ball,
A scarf will be torn from a lovely head...

But if this is life—delirium's necessity
And a forest of ships' masts—tall houses:
Then fly, armless victory,
Hyperborean plague!

On the square with the armored cars
I see a man; he
Frightens the wolves with burning torches:
Freedom, equality, legality![31]

1917

A hush that evening in the organ forest.
Then singing for us: Schubert, cradle songs,
the noise of a mill, and the voice of a storm
where the music had blue eyes and was drunk and laughing.

Brown and green is the world of the old song,
and young forever. There the maddened king
of the forest shakes the whispering crowns
of the nightingale lindens.

With darkness he returns, and his terrible strength
is wild in that song, like a black wine.
He is the Double, an empty ghost
peering mindlessly through a cold window.

1918

Wandering fire at a fearsome height,
But can a star really flicker like that?
Transparent star, wandering fire,
Your brother, Petropolis, is dying.

Dreams of earth burn at a fearsome height;
The green star flickers,
O, if you are a star, brother to water and sky,
Your brother, Petropolis, is dying.

At a fearsome height, a monstrous ship
Progresses, trimming its wings—
Green star, in beautiful poverty,
Your brother, Petropolis, is dying.

Above the black Neva transparent spring
Has burst. Immortality's wax melts.
O, if you are a star—Petropolis, your city,
Your brother, Petropolis, is dying. [32]

1918

Praise, brothers, the twilight of freedom,
The great twilight year!
Into the roiling night waters
A weighty frame of nets descends.
You'll emerge in years of muteness—
O sun; o magistrate; o people!

Praise the fateful burden,
That the people's leader, in tears, takes up.
Praise the twilight burden of power,
Its intolerable pressure.
All who have a heart must listen, o time,
As your ship heads for the sea floor.

We've bound swallows
In battle legions—look:
The sun is hidden; all nature
Twitters, stirs and is alive;
Through the netting—thick twilight—
The sun is hidden and the earth sets sail.

Well, let's give it a try: a huge, clumsy
Grinding turn of the wheel.
The earth sets sail. Take courage, men.
Dividing the ocean like a plow,
We will remember even in frigid Lethe
That this one earth cost us ten heavens.

May, 1918, Moscow

TRISTIA

I have studied the science of good-byes,
the bare-headed laments of night.
The waiting lengthens as the oxen chew.
In the town the last hour of the watch.
And I have bowed to the knell of night in the rooster's throat
when eyes red with crying picked up their burden
of sorrow and looked into the distance
and the crying of women and the Muses' song became one.

Who can tell from the sound of the word 'parting'
what kind of bereavements await us,
what the rooster promises with his loud surprise
when a light shows in the Acropolis,
dawn of a new life,
the ox still swinging his jaw in the outer passage,
or why the rooster, announcing the new life,
flaps his wings on the ramparts?

A thing I love is the action of spinning:
the shuttle fluttering back and forth, the hum of the spindle,
and look, like swan's down floating toward us,
Delia, the barefoot shepherdess, flying—
o indigence at the root of our lives,
how poor is the language of happiness!
Everything's happened before and will happen again,
but still the moment of each meeting is sweet.

Amen. The little transparent figure
lies on the clean earthen plate
like a squirrel skin being stretched.
A girl bends to study the wax.
Who are we to guess at the hell of the Greeks?
Wax for women, bronze for men:
our lot falls to us in the field, fighting,
but to them death comes as they tell fortunes.

1918

On the stony slopes of Pieria
Nine muses circled in a dance
So that their blind lyricists, like bees,
Give us mellifluous Ionic honey.
A breath of lofty air wafted from
A virginal and convex forehead
So that far-off posterity might open
The tender coffins of the archipelago.

Spring, stomping, runs down Helladic meadows,
Sappho tries on polychromatic boots
And with their ringing folksong hammers
Cicadas forge a golden folksong ring.
The carpenter raised up the roof beams high
And chickens' necks were wrung for the wedding feast,
The clumsy cobbler stretched out all five
Ox skins to carve them into shoes.

How sluggish is the lyre-tortoise!
How barely, without feet she crawls.
She lies under the sun of Epirus,
And quietly her golden belly glows.
O, who is going to be nice to her,
Who'll turn her over as she sleeps?
She even in her dreams awaits Terpander,
Longing to tremble at dry fingertips.

Oaks drink the chilly waters of a well
Amid the noise of simple-haired grass
And fragrant lungwort gladdens wasps.
O where, where are you, blessed isles,
Where no one breaks the loaf in two and bites,
Where there are only milk, honey and wine,
Where creaky labor doesn't darken heaven
And easily the wheel turns?[33]

1919

These crystal waters—so steep!
Behind us Siena's mountains preside,
And the spiky cathedrals of unbalanced cliffs
Jut in air amid wool and silence.

The organ, fortress of the Holy Spirit, progresses
Down the hanging staircase of prophets and kings,
Herd-dogs' lively barking and kind ferocity,
Herdsmen's cloaks and judges' staffs.

Here, the earth is motionless. Together with it,
I drink the cold mountain air of Christianity,
The sheer "Credo" and the caught breath of the Psalmist,
The apostolic churches' keys and rags.

What kind of line could transmit
The crystal high notes in the fortified ether?
And from the Christian mountains in astounded space,
Like a mass of Palestrina, grace descends.[34]

1919

FEODOSIA

In the ring of high hills
you stampede down your slope like sheep,
pink and white stones glistening
in the dry transparent air.
Pirate feluccas rock out at sea.
The port burns with poppies—Turkish flags.
Reed masts. The wave's resilient crystal.
Little boats on ropes like hammocks.

From morning till night, in every way possible,
everyone sings, grieving for a 'little apple.'
Its golden seed is borne away by the wind
and lost, and will never come back.
And promptly at nightfall, in the lanes,
the musicians, in twos and threes
bend and clumsily scrape
their improbable variations.

O little statues of Roman-nosed pilgrims!
O joyful Mediterranean bestiary!
Turks strut about in towels,
like roosters, by little hotels.
Dogs are moved in a small jail on wheels.
Dry dust blows in the streets,
and the vast cook from the battleship
looms cold-blooded above the market Furies.

Let's go where they've a collection of sciences,
and the art of making *shashlyk* and *chebureki*,
where the sign shows a pair of pants
to tell us what a man is.
A man's long coat, working without a head,
a barber's flying violin,
a hypnotized iron, a vision of heavenly
laundresses, smiling because it's difficult.

Here girls grow old in bangs
and ponder their curious garments.
Admirals in three-cornered hats
bring back Scheherazade's dream.
Transparent distance. A few grapevines.
A fresh wind that never drops.
And it's not far to Smyrna and Baghdad,
but it's a hard sail, and the same stars everywhere.

1920

When Psuche-life steps down into the shades'
Semitransparent wood, after Persephone—
A blind swallow swoops below
With a green bough and Stygian tenderness.

Towards the refugee rushes a crowd of shades
To lock around their new companion
As lamentations fill the air: they wring their hands
With timid hope and faint bewilderment.

One holds a mirror, another offers perfume—
The soul is female: she is charmed with trinkets—
And withered sorrows drift like drizzle in
The leafless forest of transparent voices.

And in the tender crush not knowing where to start,
The soul can't recognize those groves transparent,
Breathes on the mirror and delays handing over
The copper flatcake for the foggy crossing.

1920

I forgot the word I wished to say.
A blind swallow on clipped wings returns
To play with shades in their transparent bower.
In an unconscious swoon proceeds the night song.

Birds can't be heard. The immortelles don't bloom.
Transparent glow the manes of night herds.
In a dry river floats an empty skiff.
Among grasshoppers swoons the mindless word.

And, slowly distending as though a tent or temple,
Either impersonates mad Antigone
Or else, dead swallow, swoops below
With a green bough and Stygian tenderness.

If only to return the shame of seeing fingers
And convex joy of recognition:
I'm so afraid of the sobbing of Aonides,
Of fog, of ringing chime, of absence!

Mortals have this: to love and recognize,
For them even sound forms on fingers.
But I forgot what I had wished to say
And incorporeal thought returns to shady bowers.

Transparent one, it speaks beside the point,
It's always: girlfriend, Antigone, little swallow.
And on the lips, like black ice, burns
The recollection of the Stygian, ringing sound.

1920

We'll meet again in Petersburg
As though we had interred the sun there,
And for the first time we'll pronounce
A blessed, meaningless word.
In black velvet of Soviet night,
In velvet of world-wide emptiness,
Dear eyes of blessed women still sing;
Immortelles still bloom.

The capital, feral cat, arches its back;
A patrol stands on the bridge.
Only an angry motorcar rushes
Through the gloom, and a cuckoo calls.
I need no night pass,
And fear no sentries;
For the blessed, meaningless word
I will pray in the Soviet night.

I hear a slight, theatrical rustle
And a girlish "ah"—
And there's an enormous bunch
Of deathless roses in Kypris' hands.
We warm ourselves from boredom at the fire;
Perhaps the centuries will pass,
And the dear hands of blessed women
Will gather the weightless ashes.

Somewhere are Orpheus' sweet choruses
And dark pupils of dear eyes,
And from balconies, over flowerbeds of seats,
Playbill-doves fall.
Well then: snuff out our candles, please;
In black velvet of world-wide emptiness
Steep shoulders of blessed women still sing,
And you won't notice the night sun.

1920

Because I couldn't hold back your arms,
Because I betrayed those salty, tender lips,
I must await dawn in this impassable acropolis—
How I hate these fetid, ancient palisades.

Achaean men are equipping a horse in the gloom;
Saws' serrations cut hard into walls.
This dry agitation of blood refuses to settle down,
For you there is no name, no sound, no likeness.

How could I think that you would return? How could I dare?
Why did I pull away from you too soon?
Shadows had not yet lifted; rooster had yet to crow,
And the hot axe had yet to sink into wood.

A transparent tear, a drop of tar has formed upon the walls,
And the city senses its wooden ribs,
But the blood has rushed to the stairs and into the assault,
And the men have seen the alluring image three times in dreams.

Where is fair Troy? Where is the royal, the maiden's house?
It shall be destroyed—Priam's tall aviary.
And the arrows fall in a dry rain of wood,
While other arrows grow out of the earth like hazel.

The sting of the last star dies out painlessly,
And the morning, a grey swallow, raps against the window,
And a slow day, as an ox awakening in the straw,
Stirs in the squares, disheveled from long sleep.

1920

When the urban moon rises over the squares,
And slowly the impassable city lights up below,
And night swells, filled with sorrow and bronze,
And sonorous wax gives way to time's coarseness.

And cuckoo weeps on its stone tower
And an ashen reaping-woman, descending
To the unbreathing world, stirs shades with long spokes,
And throws yellow straw across wooden decks...

1920

Let me be in your service
like the others
mumbling predictions,
mouth dry with jealousy.
Parched tongue
thirsting, not even for the word—
for me the dry air is empty
again without you.

I'm not jealous any more
but I want you.
I carry myself like a victim
to the hangman.
I will not call you
either joy or love.
All my own blood is gone.
Something strange paces there now.

Another moment
and I will tell you:
it's not joy but torture
you give me.
I'm drawn to you
as to a crime—
to your ragged mouth,
to the soft bitten cherry.

Come back to me,
I'm frightened without you.
Never had you such power
over me as now.
Everything I desire
appears to me.
I'm not jealous any more.
I'm calling you.

1920

Into the circle dance of shades, beating down the tender meadow
I came with singing name…
But everything melted away, and only a weak sound
Remained in hazy memory.

At first, I thought that the name was a Seraph,
And was wary of its light body.
A few days passed, and I was merged with it,
Dissolving into the dear shade.

Once again, the apple tree drops a wild fruit,
And a secret image flickers before me,
And curses the deity, and damns itself,
And swallows coals of jealousy.

But happiness rolls on, a golden hoop,
Fulfilling an alien will,
And you chase after that springtime of ease,
Cutting the air with your palm.

And it's been so arranged that we never exit
This enchanted circle;
The supple hills of this virgin land
Lie tightly swaddled.

1920

1921 – 1924
Poems

CONCERT AT THE RAILWAY STATION

Can't breathe. And the firmament seething with worms,
and not one star speaking.
But as God's our witness, there's music above us—
the Aeonian maids, at whose song the station trembles,
and again the violin-laden air is sundered
and fused together by the whistles of trains.

Immense park. The station a glass sphere.
A spell cast again on the iron world.
The train carriage is borne away in state
to the echoing feast in misty Elysium.
Peacocks crying, a piano's bass notes—
I'm late. I'm afraid. This is a dream.

And I enter the station, the glass forest.
The harmony of violins is disheveled and weeping.
The savage life of the night choir,
a smell of roses from rotting beds,
where the beloved shade passed the night
under the glass sky, among the traveling crowds.

And I think, how like a beggar the iron world
shivers, covered with music and froth.
And I go out through the glass passage. The steam
blinds the pupils of the violin bows. Where are you off to?
It's the funeral feast of the beloved shade.
It's the last time the music sounds for us.[35]

1921

I washed at night in the courtyard—
The firmament shone with coarse stars.
Ray of starlight—like salt on an axe;
The barrel, brimming full, grows cold.

The gates are locked shut,
And the land is strict in conscience—
Nowhere will you find a purer base
Than the truth of fresh canvas.

A star dissolves like salt in the barrel,
And the chill water is blacker;
Death is purer, misfortune saltier,
And the earth is more righteous and terrible.

1921

No way of knowing
when this song began.
Does the thief rustle to its tune?
Does the prince of mosquitoes hum it?

O, if I could speak once more
about nothing at all,
blaze up like a struck match,
nudge night awake with my shoulder,

heave up the smothering haystack,
the muffling hat of air,
shake out the stitches
of the sack of caraway seeds,

then the pink knot of blood,
the hushing of these dry grasses
would be here in the trance after
a century, a hayloft, a dream.

1922

The wind brought comfort to us.
We could feel in the azure
dragonflies with Assyrian wings,
vibrations of the noded dark.

And the darkened sky's underside
threatened like the thunder of armies,
forest of mica membranes
flying with six-armed bodies.

There is a blind niche in the azure:
in each blessed noon
one fateful star trembles,
hinting at the depth of night.

And Azrael, among scales of crippled wings
threading his difficult way,
takes by its high arm
the defeated sky.

1922

THE AGE

My age, my animal, who will be able
To glance into your pupils
And cement together with his blood
The vertebrae of two centuries?
Blood-the-builder is gushing
From the throat of earthly things;
But a freeloader merely trembles
On the threshold of new days.

A creature, so long as life persists,
Must bear its vertebrae to the end,
And the ocean wave plays
With its invisible spine.
It's like a child's tender cartilage,
This infant age of earth.
Once again as a sacrifice, like a lamb,
They've offered up life's head.

In order to tear the age from captivity,
In order to start a new world,
The knotted joints of the day
Must be bound together by the flute.
It is the age that caresses the wave
With human melancholy,
And in the grass, the serpent breathes,
Golden measure of the age.

And buds will swell again,
A shoot of green will burst,
But your spine's been broken,
My beautiful, pitiful age!
And with a senseless smile,
Cruel and weak, you'll glance back,
Just like an animal, once lithe,
At the traces of its own paws.

Blood-the-builder is gushing
From the throat of earthly things,
And it's heaving the sea's warm cartilage,
A burning fish, against the shore.
And from the lofty bird-net,
From damp, azure cliffs,
Indifference pours and pours
Over your mortal wound.

1923

THE FINDER OF A HORSESHOE
(A Pindaric Fragment)

We look at woods and we say:
Here is a forest, for ships and for masts;
The pink pines
Stand free to their tops of bushy accretions,
They should creak in a storm
As do lone-standing stone pines
In the infuriated forestless air;
Beneath the salty heel of the wind the plumbline stands firm,
   driven sheer to the dancing deck,
And a seafarer
In the unfettered thirst of emptiness,
Dragging through the soaking hollows the fragile instrument
   of the surveyor,
Compares the rough surface of the seas
Against the attraction of the landward mass.

And inhaling the odor
Of resinous tears sweating out through the joints of the ship,
Admiring the decking,
Riveted and squared into bulkheads,
Not by the peaceful carpenter of Bethlehem but by another,
The father of voyages and seafarers' friend,
We say:
And they too once stood on dry land,
As uncomfortable as an ass's back,
At their tops oblivious of their roots
On a famous mountain ridge.
And the soughed beneath fresh torrential rains,
Unsuccessfully suggesting to heaven that their noble load
Be exchanged for a pinch of salt.

From what should we begin?
Everything splits and sways,
The air's a-tremor from comparisons.
No single word is better than any other,
The earth is buzzing with metaphor.
And light two-wheelers,
Garishly harnessed to flocks of straining birds,
Collapse in fragments,
Rivaling the snorting favorites of the tracks.

Thrice blesséd is he who enshrines a name in song,
A song embellished by a name
Lives longer than all the others;
It stands out among the rest by the frontlet on its brow,
That heals it from amnesia, from the stupefying smell:
Whether the closeness of a man
Or the odor exuded by a strong beast's coat,
Or simply the scent of savory rubbed between the palms.

Air can get as dark as water and all things in it swim like fish,
Thrusting the element past with their fins,
For it is solid, elastic, slightly warmed,
A crystal where wheels turn and horses shy,
The damp, black soil of Neaira, each night turned up anew,
By pitchforks, tridents, mattocks, ploughs;
The air's worked over as thickly as the ground:
One can't get out from it, nor easily get in.

A rustle rushes through the trees like a green racket;
But the children play at five-stones with the vertebras of dead beasts,
And the fragile chronography of our times is drawing to a close.
Thank you for that which has been:
I myself went wrong, was mistaken, made an error in my calculations;
The era echoed like a golden orb,
Hollow, cast, not supported by anyone,
And responded "Yes" and "No" to each touch
As a child can answer equally:
"I'll give you an apple" or "I shan't give you one,"
While his face is an accurate cast of his voice as he utters the words.

The sound continues to ring though the source of the sound
    has gone.
A horse lies in the dust and snorts in a sweat,
But the steep curve of its neck
Still retains remembrance of the race in its outstretched hooves
When there were not just four,
But as many hooves as stones in the road,
Redoubled in four dimensions
By the number of thuds of the ground of the racehorse seething
    with heat.
Thus
The finder of the horseshoe
Blows the dust off it
And polishes it with wool till it shines,
Then
He hangs it on his door
For it to rest,
And to free it from the need to strike sparks from flint.
Human lips with nothing more to say
Retain the shape of their last uttered word,
And a sense of heaviness stays in the hand
Though a jug being carried home has half spilled over.

That which I'm saying now is not me speaking
But has been dug from the earth like grains of fossilized wheat.
Some stamp coins with lions,
Others stamp them with heads;
All kinds of copper, bronze, and gold wafers,
Equally honored, lie in the earth.
The age has tried to chew them and left on each the clench
   of its teeth.
Time clips me like a coin
And there isn't enough of me left for myself.[36]

1923

SLATE ODE

The voices are the only hint
At what was scratching, fighting there…[37]

Star with star—potent conjunction,
The flint road from the old song,
Language of flint and air,
Flint with water, ring with horseshoe,
On the soft shale of the clouds
A milky slate drawing—
No curriculum of worlds,
But the ravings of dazed sheep.

We stand asleep in thick night
Warm in our sheepskin hats.
Backwards, into bedrock, the spring babbles
As chain, as foam and as speech.
Here, fear writes, the fault-line writes
With a milky lead pencil,
Here a draft ripens
·By students of running water.

Precipitous goat cities,
Layering more potent than flint,
But all the same, just another ridge—
Sheep churches, sheep towns!
Plumb-line reads them sermons,
Water instructs them, time sharpens them;
But every individual has long saturated
Air's transparent forest.

Like a dead drone next to the honeycomb,
Pied day is swept out in disgrace.
And night, the falcon, brings
Burning chalk to feed the stylus.
O, to wipe the day's marks
From the iconoclast slate,
And, like a nestling, shake off
Already transparent visions!

Harvest gathered, grapes ripening.
Day raged, like day rages.
And a tender game of jacks;
Fur of fierce shepherd dogs at noon.
Yet, like debris from icy heights—
The underside of green images—
Hungry water flows,
Whirling, prancing like a little beast.

And like a spider it crawls toward me,—
Where every conjunction is moon-spattered,
On a stunned precipice
I hear the shriek of slate.
I break the night, the burning chalk,
For a hard momentary inscription,
I trade noise for arrows' singing,
I trade structure for a furious hawk.

Who am I? No straight mason,
No roofer, no shipwright,—
I'm ambidextrous, with double soul,
I'm night's friend, day's spearhead.
He who named flint is blessed,
Student of running water!
Blessed is he who shod
The foot of the mountain, on terra firma!

And now I study the diary
Scratched by a slate year,
Language of flint and air,
A layer of gloom, a layer of light,
And I want to press my fingers
Into the flint road from the old song,
Into the lesion, arriving at a conjunction
Of flint with water, ring with horseshoe.[38]

1923

JANUARY 1, 1924

Whoever kissed time on its exhausted crown
With filial tenderness will then
Remember how time lay down to sleep
In the grain snowdrift past the window.
Whoever raised the century's sickly eyelids—
Two large and round sleepy apples—
Will always hear din—how roared the rivers
Of times false, deaf and dead.

Two sleepy eyes, two apples has the headman
Century, and a lovely clay mouth
But dying he shall cleaveTo the embarrassed hand of his
now aging son.
I know: each day life's exhale grows more faint.
A little longer and they'll cut
This simple tune about clay offenses
And pour lead down the throat.

O life of clay! O dying of the century!
I fear you may be known
Only by him who shows the errant smile
Of those who've lost themselves.
What a dull pain—to search for the word lost,
Raising up sickly eyelids,
With sediment in blood to gather
Night-blooming grasses for the foreign tribe.

Time: century. The sediment of lime
In sick son's blood hardens. Like a wooden case,
Sleeps Moscow. The headman century grants no place to run.
Snow smells of apples as it did before.
I want to run from my threshold.
Where to? The street is dark
And, like salt sprinkled over paving,
White conscience shows before me.

Along the byways, crooks, coops, holes,
Close by and barely, last-minute,
I, private passenger in a fish-fur coat,
Keep trying to button up the sledge rug.
One street, another glimmers past,
The sledge's crunch in the cold recalls an apple's,
The buttonhole evades the effort,
All the time slipping from the grasp.

With what metallic, iron-mongering clamor
The winter night clangs down the streets of Moscow,
Bangs like a frozen fish or whistles clouds of steam
From pink teahouses—like schools of silver roach.
Moscow. Moscow again. I say, hello,
Don't pout, it is not so bad now,
As an old acquaintance I accept the terms
Of brotherly cold and pikefish justice.

The chemist's sign raspberry-colors snow.
Somewhere the typewriter clicks and clacks.
A cabman's back. A half-a-yard of snow.
What else do you want? No one will touch you,
No one will kill you. Gorgeous is winter.
The goat sky scatters stars and shines
Like milk. The sledge rug rubs its horsehair
Against the gelid runners. It rings.

Who was it blackened crooked lanes with kerosene,
And swallowed snow, raspberry jam, ice?
They'll ever molt their scaly Soviet sonatina,
With nineteen-twenty on their tongues.
Could I betray to shameful denigration—
Again cold air smells of apples—
Oaths of allegiance to the fourth estate
And vows so great we wept?

Who else will you kill? Who else will you celebrate?
What other lies will you invent?
There's the rasp of the typewriter—quick, rip out a key!
And you'll find a pikefish bone.
That sediment of lime in sick son's blood
Will then dissolve. And he'll ring with rapt laughter.
Yet these typewriters' simple sonatina
Is just a shadow of sonatas other, greater.

1924 (1937)

No, I was no one's contemporary—ever.
That would have been above my station.
How I loathe that other with my name.
He certainly never was me.

The age is a despot with two sleepy apples
to see with, and a splendid mouth of earth.
When he dies he'll subside onto the numb
arm of his son, who's already ageing.

As the age was born I opened my red eyelids,
my eyes were large sleepy apples.
The rivers thundered, informing me
of the bloodshot lawsuits of men.

A hundred years back,
on the camp-bed, on a drift of pillows,
there was a sprawled clay body: the age
getting over its first drunk.

What a frail bed, when you think
how the world creaks on its journey.
Well, we can't forge another.
We'd better get along with this one.

In stuffy rooms, in cabs, in tents,
the age is dying. Afterwards
flames will flutter like feathers, on the apple-skins,
on the curled wafers of horn.

1924

1930 – 1934
Armenia and Moscow

Much we have to fear,
big-mouth beside me!

Our tobacco turns into dust,
nut-cracker, friend, idiot!

And I could have whistled through life like a starling,
eating nut-pies....

but clearly there's no chance of that.

1930

From the cycle "ARMENIA"

Ah, I see nothing, and my poor ear has gone deaf.
Of all the colors the only left to me are terracotta and hoarse ochre.

And for some reason I started to dream an Armenian morning;
I thought—fine, let's take a look at how the bluebird lives in
    Erevan,

At how the baker bends over, playing blind-man's-bluff with
    the bread,
Hauling from the oven moist hides of *lavash*...

Ah, Erevan, Erevan! Were you drawn by a bird,
Or did a lion color you in, like a child with a painted pencil case?

Ah, Erevan, Erevan! Not a city—but a broiled nut;
I love the crooked Babylons of your wide-mouthed streets.

I've smudged and worn my pointless life, as a Mullah his Koran,
I've frozen my time and poured out no hot blood.

Ah, Erevan, Erevan, I need nothing more;
I do not want your frozen grapes.

1930

I returned to my city, familiar as tears,
As veins, as mumps from childhood years.

You've returned here, so swallow as quick as you can
The cod-liver oil of Leningrad's riverside lamps.

Recognize when you can December's brief day:
Egg yolk folded into its ominous tar.

Petersburg, I don't yet want to die:
You have the numbers of my telephones.

Petersburg, I have addresses still
Where I can raise the voices of the dead.

I live on the backstairs and the doorbell buzz
Strikes me in the temple and tears at my flesh.

And all night long I await those dear guests of yours,
Rattling, like manacles, the chains on the doors.

December, 1930

I saw the world of power through a child's eyes—
oysters frightened me, I looked bashfully at the sentries—
I owe it not one jot of my soul:
something alien to me, which I never wanted.

I never stood under the bank's Egyptian porch,
stupidly pompous, in a beaver mitre, glowering.
Never, never, above the lemon Neva, to the rustle
of hundred rouble notes, did a gypsy girl dance for me.

Feeling executions on the way, I escaped from the roar
of rebellious events, to the Nereids on the Black Sea,
and from those days' beautiful women, gentle European women,
what anguish I consumed, what torment!

Why then does this city, even now, satisfy
my thoughts and my feelings at home in its ancient night?
It is more insolent than ever with its frost and fires,
more arrogant, damned, empty—it looks younger.

Maybe that's because, in a child's picture book,
I saw Lady Godiva draped in her red mane,
and I'm still whispering under my breath
Good-bye, Lady Godiva... Godiva, I've forgotten...

February, 1931

"Ma voix aigre et fausse…"
  —Paul Verlaine

I'll tell you bluntly
One last time:
It's only maddening cherry brandy,
Angel mine.

Where the Greeks just saw their raped
Beauty's fame,
Through black holes at me there gaped
Nought but shame.

But the Greeks hauled Helen home
In their ships.
Here a smudge of salty foam
Flecks my lips.

What rubs my lips and leaves no trace?
—Vacancy.
What thrusts a V-sign in my face?
—Vagrancy.

Quickly, wholly, or slowly as a snail,
All the same,
Mary, angel, drink your cocktail,
Down your wine.

I'll tell you bluntly
One last time:
It's only maddening cherry brandy,
Angel mine.[39]

March 2, 1931

For the sake of the future's trumpeting heroics,
for that exalted tribe,
I was robbed of my cup at my fathers' feast,
and of my laughter and honor.

The wolfhound age springs at my shoulders
though I'm no wolf by blood.
Better to be stuffed up a sleeve like a fleece cap
in a fur coat from the steppes of Siberia,

and so not see the sniveling, nor the sickly smears,
nor the bloody bones on the wheel,
so all night the blue foxes would still gleam
for me as they did in the first times.

Lead me into the night by the Yenesey
where the pine touches the star.
I'm no wolf by blood,
and only my own kind will kill me.

March 17 – 28, 1931

No, it's not for me to duck out of the mess
behind the cabdriver's back that's Moscow.
I'm the cherry swinging from the streetcar strap
of an evil time. What am I doing alive?

We'll take Streetcar A and then Streetcar B,
you and I, to see who dies first. As for Moscow,
one minute she's a crouched sparrow,
the next she's puffed up like a pastry—

how does she find time to threaten from holes?
You do as you please, I won't chance it.
My glove's not warm enough for the drive
around the whole whore Moscow.

April, 1931

I drink to military asters, to all I've been censured about,
To the aristo's fur coat, to asthma, to the jaundiced Petersburg day,

To the music of pines in Savoie, petrol on the Champs-Elysées.
To roses in a Rolls-Royce saloon, to Parisian pictures' oil paint.

I drink to the surf of Biscay, to a jug of cream from the Alps,
To English girls' redheaded hauteur, and distant colonial quinine;

I drink but still have to choose between wines:
Sparkling Asti Spumante or Châteauneuf-du-Pape.

April 11, 1931

to Anna Akhmatova

Keep my words forever for their aftertaste of misfortune and smoke,
their tar of mutual tolerance, honest tar of work.
Sweet and black should be the water of Novgorod wells
to reflect the seven fins of the Christmas star.

And in return, father, friend, rough helper, I
the unrecognized brother, outlawed from the people's family,
promise to fit the beam-cages tight to the wells
so the Tartars can lower the princes in tubs, for torture.

O ancient headsman's blocks, keep on loving me!
Players in the garden seem to aim at death, and hit nine-pins.
I walk through my life aiming like that, in my iron shirt
(why not?) and I'll find an old beheading axe in the woods.

May 3, 1931

Still far from patriarch or sage,
I'm still a half-respected age.
I still get cursed behind my back
In the savage tongue of tramcar rows,
Possessed of neither rhyme nor sense,
"What a so-and-so!" they say. I apologize,
But in my heart don't mend my ways.

If you think, you'd not believe yourself,
What ties you to the world is rubbish:
A midnight key to someone's flat,
A silver coin in your pocket
And the celluloid of a detective film.

I rush like a puppy to the phone
Every hysterical time it rings:
A Polish voice saying "Tzank you, Sur,"
A soft reproach from another town,
Some obligation unfulfilled.

You wonder what you dare to like
Amid these tricks and fireworks.
You boil over: but they won't go away—
The meddling hands of idleness—
Please get a light from them, not me.

I sometimes laugh and sometimes try
To play the gentlemen with white walking stick;
Listening to sonatas in alleyways,
I lick my lips at hawker's trays,
I leaf through books in blocky entranceways
And do not live, yet seem to live.

I visit reporters and sparrows,
I go to a street photographer:
In no time he gets out of a bucket
An adequate likeness of me
Against Shah Mountain's lilac cone.

And sometimes I run off on errands
To airless cellars filled with steam
Where Chinamen, honest and clean,
Use chopsticks to pick at paste balls
And drink vodka like swallows from the Yang-Tze.

And I love the squeaking trams' departures
And the asphalt's Astrakhan caviar
All covered in straw like matting;
It reminds me of basket work on Asti
And the ostrich fans of building-yard junk
When the Leninist houses first rise.

I enter puppet-theater museums
Where opulent Rembrandts swell,
Now glazed like Cordova leather
I marvel at Titian's horned miters
And Tintoretto's bright tints I admire
For their myriad screaming parakeets....

But how I'd love to speak my mind,
To play the fool, to spit out truth,
Send spleen to the dogs, to the devil, to hell,
Take someone's arm and say, "Be so kind,
I think your way lies the same as mine."

May – September, 1931

LAMARCK

There was an old man shy as a boy,
a gawky, timid patriarch—
who picked up the challenge for the honor of nature?
Who else? The man of passion, Lamarck.

If all that's alive is no more than a blot
for the brief escheated day,
give me the last rung
on Lamarck's moving ladder.

I'll hiss my way down through the lizards and snakes
to the annelid worms and the sea-slugs,
across resilient gangways, through valleys,
I'll shrink, and vanish, like Proteus.

I'll put on a shell cloak,
I'll be done with warm blood,
I'll grow suckers, I'll sink feelers
into the foam of the sea.

We went through the classes of insects
with their liquid liqueur-glass eyes.
He said, "Nature's a shambles.
There's no vision. You're seeing for the last time."

He said, "No more harmony.
In vain you loved Mozart.
Now comes the deafness of spiders.
Here is ruin stronger than our strength.

Nature has gone away from us
as though she didn't need us.
She's slid the oblong brain
into a dark sheath, like a sword.

She's forgotten the drawbridge.
She lowered it late
for those with a green grave,
red breath, sinuous laughter…"

May 7 – 9, 1932

IMPRESSIONISM

The artist has depicted for us
A profound daze of lilac
And has put resonant steps of colors,
Scaly crust, onto canvas.

He understood oil's density;
Its baked-over summer
Was heated by a mauve brain,
And expanded in stifling heat.

But the shading, that shading—ever more mauve;
A whistle or whip is snuffed out like a match.
You'd say: cooks in the kitchen
Are preparing plump pigeons.

One guesses at the swing,
Veils barely sketched in;
And in this twilight wreckage
The bumblebee is already master.

May 23, 1932

TO THE GERMAN TONGUE
to B. S. Kuzin[40]

Killing myself, contradicting myself,
A moth flying towards a midnight flame,
I want to exit our language
Because of all I owe it on endless credit.

Between us there is praise without flattery,
And fast friendship, without hypocrisy;
Let's study solemnity and honor
From a foreign family in the West.

Thunderstorms do you good, poetry!
I recall a German officer:
Roses climbed the hilt of his sword
And Ceres was on his lips.

Frankfurt's fathers were only just yawning,
There was still no news of Goethe,
They were composing hymns, horses caracoled
And pranced in place like letters.

Tell me, friends, in what Valhalla
Did we crack nuts together,
What was that freedom you possessed,
What signposts did you place for me?

And straight from the page of an almanac,
From its first-order novelty,
We rushed into the grave, fearless down the steps,
As though to the cellar for a glass of Moselle.

The foreign tongue will cover me like skin;
Long before I ventured to be born,
I was a letter, a line of grapevines,
I was the very book you're dreaming of.

When I slept without face or character,
Friendship woke me like a shot.
God-Nachtigal, grant me Pylades' fate
Or tear out my tongue—I don't need it.

God-Nachtigal, they're recruiting me still
For new plagues, for seven-year slaughters.
Sound has thinned. Words hiss, rebel,
But you live on and with you I am calm. [41]

August 8 – 12, 1932

ARIOSTO

Ariosto—no one in Italy more delightful—
these days has a frog in his throat.
He amuses himself with the names of fish,
he rains nonsense into the seas.

Like a musician with ten cymbals,
forever breaking in on his own music,
he leads us backwards and forwards, himself quite lost
in the maze of chivalric scandals.

A Pushkin in the language of the cicadas,
with a Mediterranean haughtiness to his melancholy,
he leaves his hero struggling with the preposterous,
and shudders, and is another man.

He says to the sea: roar but don't think!
To the maiden on the rock: lie there without bedclothes!
We've heard too little—tell us again,
while there's blood in the veins, and a roar in the ears.

O lizard city with a crust for a heart, and no soul.
Ferrara, give birth to more of such men!
While there's blood in the veins, hurry, tell the story
so often told, once more from the beginning.

It's cold in Europe. Italy is in darkness.
And power—it's like having to swallow a barber's hand.
But he goes on improving his act, playing
the great man smiling out of the window

at the lamb on the hill, the monk on his donkey,
the Duke's men-at-arms silly with wine
and the plague and garlic,
the baby dozing under a net of flies.

I love his desperate leisure,
his babble, the salt and sugar of his words,
the sounds happily conspiring in twos and threes.
Why should I want to split the pearl?

Ariosto, maybe this age will vanish
and we'll pour your azure and our Black Sea together
into one wide fraternal blue.
We too know it well. We've drunk mead on its shore.[42]

May 4 – 6, 1933

Don't push your luck with foreign tongues—try to forget them:
All the same you won't bite through glass with your teeth!

Respect for foreign twitter comes with such torment:
Illegal raptures are deterred by severe price!

Truly, the dying body and thinking, immortal mouth
Won't be saved by uttering a foreign name one last time
    before parting.

What if the Ariosto and Tasso who enthrall us
Are monsters with deep-blue brains and fish-scales made of
    moist eyes?

And as punishment for pride, unrepentant lover of sounds,
You will receive a vinegar sponge to clench with traitorous lips.

May, 1933

The apartment's dumb as paper,
it emptied by itself.
Sounds start slithering
through the radiator.

Our estate's in order:
telephone frozen into frog,
all our veteran possessions
homesick for the street.

A damnation of flimsy walls.
Nowhere to run to.
I'll have to play tunes on a comb
for somebody, like a clown.

Tunes ruder than students sing,
more insolent than young party members,
but I have to teach the hangmen,
perched on their school-bench, bird-notes.

I read ration-books.
I catch phrases like nooses.
I sing warning lullabies
to the rich peasant's good child.

Someone who draws from the life,
some fine-comb of the flax collective,
someone with blood in his ink
ought to sit on this stake.

Some respected informer, left
like salt when a purge boiled away,
some family's breadwinner
ought to crush this moth.

What teeth of malice lurking
in every detail,
as though Nekrasov's hammer
were still nailing the nails.

Let's start as though we were stretched
on the headsman's block, you and I,
on the other side of seventy years.
Old loafer, it's time for you to stamp your boots.

It won't be the fountain Hippocrene
that will burst through the hack-work walls,
but the current of household terror
in this evil coop in Moscow.[43]

November, 1933

We live, not feeling the land beneath us;
Our speech can't be heard ten paces away.
And wherever enough gather for half a conversation—
They mention the Kremlin mountain man.
His meaty fingers are fat as worms,
And his words are solid as ten-pound weights.
His cockroach whiskers laugh,
And his boot-tops shine.

And around him—a swarm of thin-necked leaders.
He toys with the services of half-men.
One whistles, one meows, one whimpers,
But he alone points and slams.
He forges decree after decree like horseshoes—
Hitting one in the groin; another in temple, brow or eye.
For him—every execution is sweetness,
And the broad chest of an Osetian.[44]

1933

From the cycle "OCTAVES"

III

O butterfly, o Muslim,
In a split shroud of muslin,
So living, so dying,
So giant, so as you are!

Your burnoose is over your head
With its large, hairy proboscis.
O shroud spread out like a flag,
Fold your wings—I'm frightened!

VII

Even Schubert on the wave, even Mozart in the aviary,
Even Goethe whistling on a twisting path,
Even Hamlet cutting thoughts with timorous steps
Counted the masses' pulse and believed the many.
Perhaps the whisper came before the lips
And leaves had spiraled in the treelessness,
And those to whom we consecrate experience
Formed features prior to experience.

VIII

Even the toothy paw of the maple
On round corners falls,
And you can, with butterfly speckle,
Form figures on walls.

There are mosques that are living
And I now hazard a guess:
All we are is Hagia Sophia
With an infinite many of eyes.

IX

Tell me, surveyor of deserts,
Geometer of Arabic sands,
Can it be that propulsion of lines
Overpowers the blowing wind?
"I do not care for its shuddering
Anxious Judaic patter:
It moulds matter out of mutter
And drinks mutter out of matter."

1933 – 1934

From the cycle "FROM PETRARCH"

I

> Valle che de'lamenti miei se' piena…
> —Petrarch

This river, swollen with salty tears,
And the forest birds could tell a tale,
Alert beasts and mute fishes,
Clasped between green banks;

Valley full of oaths and white-hot whispers,
Twists of ant-ridden paths,
Boulders, hardened by love's force
And fissures in earth, on rough slopes:

The unshakable is shaken in its place,
And I am shaken… As though in a core of granite
Anguish germinates in a nest of former joys,

Where I seek traces of beauty and honor
That has vanished—a falcon after feeding,
Leaving just a carcass in a bed of earth.[45]

December, 1933 – January, 1934

to the memory of Andrey Bely[46]

Blue eyes, and the bone of the forehead glowing—
the venom of the world that renews its youth was your guide.

And for the great magic that was to be yours
you were never to judge, never to curse.

They crowned you with a divine dunce-cap,
turquoise teacher, torturer, tyrant, fool.

A Gogol-ghost exploded like a blizzard in Moscow,
whirling, dense, clear, and unknowable.

With your collection of space and diploma of feathers,
author, young goldfinch, student, little student, sleighbell,

ice-skater, first-born, the age hauled you by the scruff
through new cases of words, still asleep under the snow.

Often one writes "execution" and pronounces it "song."
Some ailments simplicity may have stung to death.

But our minds don't go off with a popgun straightness.
It's not the paper but the news that saves us.

As dragonflies, missing the water, land in the reeds,
so the fat pencils settled into the dead man,

sheets were unfolded on knees for our glorious future,
and they drew, apologizing to every line.

Between you and the country a link of ice is forming,
so lie there and grow young, and never melt

and let those to come, the young, let them never inquire
what it's like for you lying there, orphan, in the clean void.

January 10 – 11, 1934

1934 – 1937
Voronezh

What is the name of this street?
Mandelstam Street.
What the hell kind of name is that?
No matter how you turn it round,
It has a crooked sound, it isn't straight.

There wasn't much about him straight,
His attitudes weren't lily-white.
And that's why this street
Or better still, this hole
Was given its name after him:
This Mandelstam.

April, 1935

I

How dark it gets along the Kama.
The cities kneel by the river on oaken knees.

Draped in cobwebs, beard with beard,
black firs and their reflections run back into their childhood.

The water leaned into fifty-two pairs of oars,
pushed them upstream, downstream, to Kazan and Cherdyn.

There I floated with a curtain across the window,
a curtain across the window, and the flame inside was my head.

And my wife was with me there five nights without sleeping,
five nights awake keeping an eye on the guards.

II

I left with the evergreen east in my eyes.
The Kama and its riches dragged at the buoy.

Let me cut the hill and its campfires into layers.
There'll be no time to grow forests.

Let me settle here, right here.
Some people live here. The Urals live on and on.

Let me take this mirror country lying on its back
and button a long coat over it and keep it warm.[47]

May – April, 1935

STANZAS

I

I don't want to pay down the last penny of my soul
among hothouse adolescents. I go to the world
as the single peasant goes to the collective
and I find the people good.

II

I'm for the Red Army style overcoat,
down to the heels, simple flat sleeves,
cut like a rain cloud over the Volga,
to hang full on the chest, one fold down the back,
no stuff wasted on double hems;
you can roll it up in the summer.

III

A damned seam, a foolishness,
came between us. Now let it be clear:
I have to live, breathing and bolshevescent.
I'll be better-looking before I die,
staying to play among the people.

IV

When you think how I raced around
in a seven-inch sweat, in dear old Cherdyn,
among the bell-bottomed river smells,
not stopping to watch the goat squabbles—
a rooster in the transparent summer night.
Grub and spit, and something, and babble—and got
the woodpecker off my back. One jump—then sane again.

V

And you my sister Moscow, how light you are,
coming to meet your brother's plane
before the first street-car bell.
You are gentler than the sea, you tossed salad
of wood, glass, milk.

VI

Once my country talked with me,
indulged me, scolded me a little, never read me.
But when I grew up and was a witness
she noticed me all at once, and like a lens
set me alight with one flash from the Admiralty.

VII

I have to live, breathing and bolshevescent,
laboring with language, disobeying, I and one other.
I hear the Arctic throbbing with Soviet pistons.
I remember everything—the necks of German brothers,
the gardener-executioner whose pastime
was the Lorelei's lilac comb.

VIII

I'm not robbed blind, not desperate,
just, only, merely, thrown.
When my string's tuned tight as Igor's song,
when I get my breath back, you can hear
in my voice the earth, my last weapon,
the dry dampness of acres of black earth.[48]

May – July, 1935

I will return this borrowed dust to the earth
Not as a floury white butterfly—
I want this thinking body
To turn into a street, a country:
A scorched, vertebrate body,
Aware of its own length.

The cries of dark green pine,
Wreaths in the well-depths,
Draw out life and precious time,
Resting on the funeral biers—
Loops of pine bound with red,
Letter-like, large wreaths.

These comrades from the final draft
Reported to work in harsh skies;
In silence, the infantry carried past
Exclamations of rifles on shoulders.

And thousands of guns at zenith—
Of black or blue eyes—
Marched in disarray—men, men, men—
Who will come after them?

July 21, 1935 – May 30, 1936

My goldfinch, I'll tip my head back—
Let's look at the world together:
Winter day, prickly like chaff;
Is it as harsh to your eye?

Boat-like tail, feathers yellow-black,
Daubed with color below the beak,
Do you know how fully you are goldfinch,
And how fully goldfinched up?

What loft there is in his forehead—
Black and red, yellow and white!
He's looking sharp both ways, both sides.
And without a glance—he flies!

December 9 – 27, 1936

It's not mine or yours. It's theirs—
All the force of blood-lines' endings:
The reed is sonorous and notched with their air,
And the snails of human lips gratefully
Take on their breathing weight.
They are nameless. Enter into their fiber
And you will inherit their kingdoms—

And for people, for their living hearts,
Wandering in those convolutions and twistings,
You will express both their pleasures
And their torments, in tides high and low.

December 9 – 27, 1936

Within the mountain the idol is still
In chambers secure, vast and blissful,
And necklaces of fat drip from his neck,
Guarding sleep's tides high and low.

When he was a boy and the peacock played with him,
He was fed on rainbow of India,
Given milk from pinkish earthen vessels
Without sparing the carmine.

The sedated bone is tied with a knot,
Knees, arms and shoulders become human.
He smiles with a mouth most serene;
He thinks by bone and feels by skull
And strives to recall his human form.

December 10 – 26, 1936

I'm in the heart of ages. The path's obscure,
But time pushes off the destination—
And the weary ash of the staff,
And the humble corrosion of bronze.

December 14, 1936

You're not dead yet. You're not yet alone,
As long as you, with your beggar-girlfriend,
Take pleasure in ravines' grandeur,
And in the gloom, the cold, the blizzard.

In luxurious poverty, potent want,
Live, calm and comforted—
Those days and nights are blessed,
And sweet-voiced labor is without sin.

He is unhappy, who, like his own shadow,
Is frightened by dog's snarl and cut by wind;
And pitiful is he, who, himself half alive,
Asks a shade for charity.

January 15 – 16, 1937

What can we do with the plains' beaten weight?
No one can believe the slow hunger in them.
We think it's theirs, the vast flatness, but on the journey
to sleep, there it is in ourselves, there it is.

Farther and farther the question spreads—where are they going
and coming from? And crawling across them
is that not the one whose name we shriek in our sleep—
the Judas of nations unborn?

January 16, 1937

Now I'm in the spider-web of light.
The people with all the shadows of their hair
need light and the pale blue air
and bread, and snow from the peak of Elbrus.

And there's no one I can ask about it.
Alone, where would I look?
These clear stones weeping themselves
come from no mountains of ours.

The people need poetry that will be their own secret
to keep them awake forever,
and bathe them in the bright-haired wave
of its breathing. [49]

January 19, 1937

If I took up charcoal to offer highest praise
In a drawing of incontestable joy,
I'd sketch the air in cunning angles,
Both carefully and anxiously.
So that the present would resound in the features
With an artistry bordering on insolence,
I'd tell of him who moved earth's axis, with reverence
For the custom of a hundred and forty nations.
I'd raise the slightest corner of one brow,
And raise it yet again in different resolution;
Pay heed: Prometheus has blown his coal alight!
Attend, Aeschylus: as I draw, I weep!

I'd grasp a few explosive lines,
His entire young millennium,
And courage I'd bind with a smile,
And then release in unperturbed light.
And in wise eyes' friendship I'd discover
An expression for my unspoken twin. Draw near
To it, to him, and suddenly you'll know your father
And gasp, feeling the world's proximity.
And I want to thank the hills,
For developing this bone, this vine:
He was born in the mountains and knew prison's sorrow.
I want to name him—not Stalin—Dzhugashvili!

Artist, preserve and protect the warrior:
Surround him in his height with a rough, azure grove
Of humid attention. Do not offend the father
With base image or shortfall of thought.
Artist, aid the one who is entirely with you,
Who thinks, feels and builds.
Not I, not some other—the people are dear to him.
The Homer-people will increase his praises threefold.
Artist, preserve and protect the warrior:
A forest of humanity, growing denser, follows him;
The future itself is in the wise man's train,
Obeying him with ever greater pace and fervor.

As from a mountain, he hung down off the tribunal
Among mounds of heads. Debtor trumps claimant.
Those potent eyes are resolutely kind;
The thick brow shines out to someone near.
And I'd like to indicate with an arrow
That firm mouth—father of direct talk.
That sculpted, complex, steep eyelid; see:
It works out of a million frames.
He is all frankness; all bronze of recognition
And acute hearing that doesn't miss a sourdine.
To all who are ready to live and die
These somber creases flash and play.

Clutching the charcoal that has brought all together,
Summoning a mere likeness with a greedy hand,
With a predatory hand, to capture likeness' axis,
I pulverize the coal, searching out his image.
I am his student—not studying for myself,
I am his student—have no mercy for yourself.
Do misfortunes conceal a part of the great plan?
I will search it out among their offspring's accidents...
So what if I am still unworthy of friends,
So what if I am not yet full of bile and tears—
I still dream of him in overcoat and cap
On that fabled square with joyous eyes.

Stalin's eyes divide the mountain
And narrow the valley in the distance,
Like an unperturbed sea, a tomorrow out of yesterday—
Furrows right up to the sun from a giant plow.
He smiles the smile of a reaper
Of hands clasped in conversation,
Who began and continues without end
On the open plain of a sixfold oath.
And every bushel, every bale
Is strong, compact, smart—a living good—
A miracle of the people! Let life be large!
The pivot of happiness shifts.

And six times over I preserve in consciousness,
Slow witness of labor, battle and harvest,
His enormous path—through taiga
And Lenin's October—to the oath fulfilled.
Mounds of human heads recede into the distance:
And I fade away there. I won't be noticed.
But in kind books and children's games
I'll rise from death to tell of the shining sun.
There is no fuller truth than warrior's frankness.
For honor and love, for air and steel
There is a glorious name for strong lips to read.
We have heard and we have found that name.[50]

January – February, 1937

Rifts of rounded bays, and flint, and blue,
And the slow sail, completed by a cloud—
I'm separated from you, having barely known you:
Longer than organ fugues—sea grass is bitter,
False tresses—and the scent of drawn-out lies,
Going to the head with iron tenderness,
And the slightly sloping shore gnawing rust...
How has this other sand been placed beneath my head?
You, throaty Urals, broad-shouldered Volga region
Or this flat land—these are my entitlements,
And I must still breathe them in with full chest. [51]

February 4, 1937

Armed with the sight of the fine wasps
sucking at the earth's axis, the earth's axis,
I recall each thing that I've had to meet,
I remember it by heart, and in vain.

I do not draw or sing
or ply the dark-voiced bow.
I make a little hole in life. How I envy
the strength and cunning of the wasps!

Oh if only once the sting of the air and the heat
of summer could make me hear
beyond sleep and death
the earth's axis, the earth's axis.

February 8, 1937

POEMS ABOUT THE UNKNOWN SOLDIER

1.

Let this air bear witness,
Its long-range heart,
And in dug-outs, omnivorous and efficient,
A windowless ocean—materiality.

These stars are such informants!
They must see all—and for what?—
For the censure of judge and witness,
For the windowless ocean—materiality…

The rain, discourteous planter, recalls,
Its unnamed manna,
The forest of crosses inscribed
On ocean or battle formation.

People, cold and sickly,
Will kill, grow cold, hunger—
And into his famed tomb
The unknown soldier is laid.

Instruct me, sickly swallow
Who has unlearned flight,
How can I cope with this aerial tomb
Without rudder or wing?

And for Mikhail Lermontov
I will give you a strict accounting
Of how the grave alone straightens the hunchback
And how the aerial trough beckons.

2.

Trembling grapes—
These worlds menace us;
And captured cities,
Golden blunders, slanders,
And the fruits of poisonous chills hang
In the pavilion of stretched constellations—
Amid the golden oils of constellations.

3.

An Arabian muddle, a rubble,
The light of velocities ground into rays;
And a ray stands with crooked soles
Upon my retina.

Millions, killed for nothing,
Trampled out a path in nothingness—
In the name of the earthworks:
A good night, all the best to them.

Uncorrupted sky of trenches,
Sky of massive, wholesale deaths,
Beyond you, past you, all of you
My lips carry me onward in darkness—

Past the shell craters, levees, slag hills,
Over which he lingered and dimmed—
The dismal, poxed and smoky
Spirit of blown open graves.

4.

The infantry dies well,
And the night chorus sings well
Over snub-nosed Schweik's smile
And over Don Quixote's avian lance
And over the knight's avian tarsus.
And cripple is friend to man—
Work will be found for them both;
And rattling at the century's extremes
The kinship of wooden crutches—
Hey, brothers—it spans the globe!

5.

Could it be that the skull extends out
Across the entire brow, temple to temple,
So that armies will be unable
To resist pouring into its precious orbits?
From life, the skull extends
Across the entire brow, temple to temple,
And taunts itself with its own tidy seams,
Grows bright, a reasoning cupola,
Froths with thought, seeing itself in dreams—
Cup of cups and fatherland to fatherlands—
Bonnet sewn with a pleat of stars—
Bonnet of luck—Shakespeare's sire…

6.

Aspen lucidity, sycamore vigilance
Rushes home, slightly reddish,
As though glutting with fainting spells
Both skies and their dull flame.

The excessive alone is our ally,
Ahead lies not collapse but reconnoiter;
And to struggle for life-giving air—
This glory is not for everyone.

And glutting my consciousness
With half-dazed being,
Do I have any choice but to drink this brew,
To devour my own head under fire?

For what was this packaging of wonder
Prepared in empty space,
If white stars, slightly reddish
Are rushing back home?

Step mother of the stars' encampment, night,
Can you sense what will be both now and after?

7.

The aortas grow taut with blood,
And a whisper sounds in the ranks:
"I was born in ninety-four..."
"I was born in ninety-two..."
And clutching in my fist my frayed
Year of birth, with the swarm, the herd,
I whisper with bloodless mouth:
I was born in the night from the second to third
Of January, in the ninety-first
Precarious year, and the centuries
Surround me with fire.[52]

March 2, 1937 – 1938

Maybe this is the beginning of madness.
Maybe it's your conscience:
a knot of life in which we are seized and known
and untied for existence.

So in cathedrals of crystals not found on earth
the prudent spider of light
draws the ribs apart and gathers them again
into one bundle.

And gathered together by one thin beam
the bundles of pure lines give thanks.
One day they will meet, they will assemble
like guests with the visors up,

and here on earth, not in heaven,
as in a house filled with music,
if only we don't offend them, or frighten them away.
How good to live to see it!

Forgive me for what I am saying.
Read it to me quietly, quietly.

March 15, 1937

How I wish I could fly
where no one could see me,
behind the ray of light
leaving no trace.

But you—let the light encircle you.
That's the one happiness.
Learn from a star the meaning
of light.

If it's a ray, if it's light,
that's only because
the whisper and chatter of lovers
strengthen and warm it.

And I want to tell you
that I'm whispering,
I'm giving you to the ray,
little one, in whispers.

March 27, 1937

I

To empty earth falling unwilled,
With sweet uneven gait, she goes,
Just barely keeping ahead
Of a quick girl and young brother.
She is propelled by the stifled freedom
Of inspiring deficiency;
And, perhaps, a lucent conjecture
Delaying in her gait:
About how spring's weather
Is, for us, mother to the tomb,
And this, eternal, ever begins.

II

There are women native to raw earth,
Whose every step is resonant sobbing,
To escort the resurrected and be first
To greet the dead is their calling.
And to demand their affection is criminal,
And to leave them is beyond all strength.
Today—angel, tomorrow—graveyard worm,
And the day after—just a sketch...
What was—footstep—will step beyond reach...
Flowers are deathless. Sky can't be bought.
And all that will be is just a promise.

May 4, 1937

Notes and Credits

POEM TRANSLATIONS

Charles Bernstein and Kevin M. F. Platt

Eugene Ostashevsky

Bob Perelman and Kevin M. F. Platt

Clarence Brown and W. S. Merwin

ENDNOTES

[1] O. E. Mandel'shtam, "Slovo i kul'tura" ("The Word and Culture") in his *Ob iskusstve* (Moscow: Iskusstvo, 1995), 203. Unless otherwise noted, translations in this essay are those of the author.

[2] Numbers in parentheses refer to the page numbers of cited poems in this collection.

[3] Mandel'shtam, "Utro Akmeizma" ("The Morning of Acmeism") in his *Ob iskusstve*, 186.

[4] Anna Lawton, ed., *Russian Futurism through its Manifestoes, 1912-1928*, Anna Lawton and Herbert Eagle, trans. (Ithaca, N.Y.: Cornell UP, 1988), 51.

[5] Vladimir Mayakovsky, *The Bedbug and Selected Poetry*, Patricia Blake, ed., Max Hayward and George Reavy, trans. (Bloomington: Indiana UP), 57.

[6] Cited in: Amanda Haight, *Anna Akhmatova: A Poetic Pilgrimage* (London: Oxford UP, 1976), 71.

[7] L. D. Trotskii, *Literatura i revoliutsiia* (Moscow: Politizdat, 1991), 136.

[8] My interpretation of this poem relies on: Gregory Freidin, *A Coat of Many Colors: Osip Mandelstam and His Mythologies of Self-Presentation* (Berkeley: U of California Press, 1987), 78-80; Clare Cavanagh, *Osip Mandelstam and the Modernist Creation of Tradition* (Princeton, N. J.: Princeton UP, 1995), 128-135.

[9] Mandel'shtam, "Slovo i kul'tura," 203.

[10] Cavanagh, *Osip Mandelstam*, 3-28. For Eliot's most well known statement on originality and tradition, see: T. S. Eliot, "Tradition and the Individual Talent," in his *The Sacred Wood* (London: Methuen, 1920), 42-53.

[11] Mandel'shtam, "Slovo i kul'tura," 204.

[12] Karl Marx, "The Eighteenth Brumaire of Louis Bonaparte," in *The Marx–Engels Reader*, Robert C. Tucker, ed. 2nd ed. (New York: W.W. Norton & Co., 1978), 595.

[13] O. E. Mandel'shtam, "Shum vremeni" ("The Noise of Time") in his *Ob iskusstve*, 37.

[14] Joseph Brodsky, "Introduction," in: Osip Mandelstam, *50 Poems*, Bernard Meares, trans. (New York: Persea Books, 1977), 12.

[15] Cited in Cavanagh, *Osip Mandelstam*, 6.

[16] Mandel'shtam, "Utro Akmeizma," 187-190.

[17] M. L. Gasparov, "Poet i kul'tura: Tri poetiki Osipa Mandel'shtama," in O. E. Mandel'shtam, *Polnoe sobranie stikhotvorenii* (Novaia biblioteka poeta, Bol'shaia seriia), A. G. Mets, ed. (St. Petersburg: Akademicheskii proekt, 1997), 5-64.

[18] A. A. Akhmatova, "Listki iz dnevnika," *Voprosy literatury*, No. 2 (1989), 203.

[19] Gasparov, "Poet i kul'tura," 50.

[20] Brown's and Merwin's work is from: Osip Mandelstam, *Selected Poems*, Clarence Brown and W. S. Merwin, trans. (New York: Atheneum, 1974). Meares' translations are from: Albert C. Todd, Max Hayward and Daniel Weissbort, eds., *Twentieth Century Russian Poetry: Silver and Steel: an Anthology*, selected by Yevgeny Yevtushenko (New York: Doubleday, 1993). They have been previous reprinted in: Osip Mandelstam, *50 Poems*, Bernard Meares, trans. (New York: Persea Books, 1977).

[21] Osip Mandel'shtam, *Polnoe sobranie stikhotvorenii* (Novaia biblioteka poeta, Bol'shaia seriia), A. G. Mets, ed. (St. Petersburg: Akademicheskii proekt, 1997).

[22] Attentive readers will note that poems translated by Brown and Merwin are printed without capitalization of the initial letters of each line, except where demanded by grammar. In distinction, poems translated by all other translators included in this volume capitalize the beginnings of each line. This typographical choice reflects the decisions of the translators—in Brown and Merwin's case, it corresponds closely to Merwin's own poetic practices and voice. Mandelstam, like most Russian poets, printed his works n the original with initial capitalization of lines.

[23] Nikolai S. Gumilev (1886-1921), one of the founders of the Acmeist school of poetry, a literary ally and friend of Mandelstam. Onegin refers to the title character of the Russian Romantic poet Alexander S. Pushkin's novel in verse *Evgeny Onegin*. However, Mandelstam's reference in the final stanza to Evgeny evokes the main protagonist of one of Pushkin's other works, "The Bronze Horseman." Mandelstam partially conflates the two characters.

[24] The Admiralty is the naval headquarters built at the order of Peter the Great (reigned 1682-1725) in St. Petersburg, the new capital that he founded in order to transform Russia into a European sea power.

[25] On Mandelstam's relationship to the poet Anna Akhmatova, see the introduction. Eliza Rachel (1821-1858), French Jewish actress who performed to great acclaim in the role of Phèdre in Racine's tragedy of that name.

[26] Marina Tsvetaeva (1892-1941), prominent Russian poet. Mandelstam was romantically involved with her in 1916. Uglich, the site of the death of the Tsarevich Dmitry, heir of Ivan IV of Muscovy. Boris Godunov was suspected of murdering the royal child. "Three lighted candles... There will be no fourth." A reference to the Old Russian conception of Moscow as "the third Rome," after Rome itself and Constantinople; the original formulation concludes "and there will be no fourth." In the final stanza, Mandelstam conflates his own lyric voice with the false Dmitry, a pretender to the throne whose body was burned.

[27] Petropolis, a common poetic variant name for St. Petersburg.

[28] Mandelstam's mother died on June 26, 1916. Here, Mandelstam projects this event of his personal biography against the death of an imaginary Jewish mother, a follower of Christ, living through the Crucifixion; the "black sun" refers to an eclipse during that event.

[29] The poem is devoted to Salomea N. Andronikova (1888-1982), a Georgian princess whose circle in St. Petersburg included a number of poets, including Mandelstam and Akhmatova, who called her Salomka. Salominka, or little straw, is a diminutive nickname. Mandelstam plays on her name and identity, identifying her with the biblical Salome, with Eleonora and Ligeia, the heroines of works by Edgar Allen Poe, and with Seraphite, a Balzac heroine.

[30] Anton V. Kartashev (1875-1960), to whom the poem is dedicated, was an Orthodox thinker inclined towards religious reform. In the Provisional government of 1917 (before the Bolshevik coup of October 1917) he was Minister of Religion.

[31] The poem reflects Mandelstam's initially antagonistic reaction to the Bolshevik revolution of October 1917.

[32] Petropolis, a common poetic variant name for St. Petersburg.

[33] The poem relates to the beginning of Osip and Nadezhda Mandelstam's romance and (common law) marriage.

[34] Giovanni Pierluigi da Palestrina (cir. 1524-1594), Italian Renaissance composer responsible for important reforms in liturgical music. His compositions are credited with "saving" polyphonic music from reforms initiated at the Council of Trent (1545-1563).

[35] The scene described here relates to musical concerts at the Pavlovsk railway station that Mandelstam attended in his childhood. See the first chapter of his autobiography *The Noise of Time*.

[36] Pindar, ancient Greek poet of the fifth century B.C.E.

[37] In an intriguing self-referential gesture, Mandelstam takes as epigraph to the final version of the poem a couplet that he excised from an earlier published version of this same poem.

[38] This poem contains a number of intertextual references to classic Russian poetry that are obvious to any educated Russian reader. Most important are: G. R. Derzhavin's final, uncompleted ode on mortal impermanence (1816), founded on an image of the river of time, which the poet sketched out on a slate tablet on his deathbed; and M. Iu. Lermontov's poem "I set out alone on the road..." (1841), the "old song" to which Mandelstam refers, which includes the image of the "flint road" and of a conversation of "star with star."

[39] The epigraph is from the poem "Serenade" by Paul Verlaine (1844-1896). In English translation: "My voice is piercing and false."

[40] Boris Sergeevich Kuzin (1903-1973), a biologist and friend of Mandelstam from 1930 until the poet's death.

[41] The "German officer" of the poem is Ewald Christian von Kleist (1715-1759), one of the first representatives of German Sentimentalism, whose poem "spring" called for an end to war. Nevertheless, he died in battle during the Seven Years' War.

[42] Ludovico Ariosto (1474-1533), Italian Renaissance poet.

[43] N. A. Nekrasov (1821-1878), important Russian civic poet.

[44] As detailed in the introduction, this poem was the instigation for Mandelstam's first arrest in 1934.

[45] In 1933 and 1934 Mandelstam rendered a number of Petrarch's sonnets in Russian versions that are so original that most editions of Mandelstam count them as original poems in their own right. This is the first of Mandelstam's cycle. The epigraph is the first line of the corresponding Petrarch text, sonnet CCCI "Vale, that fills up with my tears...."

[46] Andrey Bely (1880-1934), leading Russian symbolist poet and prose author.

[47] The Kama river forms part of the route of Mandelstam's initial exile in 1934 to the town of Cherdyn in the Urals.

[48] "One jump, then sane again" refers to Mandelstam's attempt to commit suicide by leaping from a window during a psychotic attack shortly after his exile in 1934. On the Admiralty, see note 23. The Song of Igor is an important early Slavic epic poem.

[49] Elbrus is the highest mountain in the Caucasus mountain range.

[50] Mandelstam's ode to Stalin was written in an attempt to save himself from political persecution. Dzhugashvili was Stalin's birth name. See this volume's Introduction.

[51] The poem is composed of reminiscences of the Crimean shore.

[52] Mandelstam worked on "Verses on the Unknown Soldier" from early March, 1937, until his arrest in May, 1938. The work contains references to the Napoleonic Wars and to the horrific trench warfare of WWI, and warns against the eruption of a new total war in Europe. Anticipation of broad conflict with fascism was widespread in Russia and Europe during the middle thirties, as Germany rebuilt its armies and civil war raged in Spain. M. Iu. Lermontov (1814-1841) was a soldier poet of the early nineteenth-century.

First published in softcover in the United States of America by Whale and Star, Delray Beach, Florida and Santa Monica, California, info@whaleandstar.com, www.whaleandstar.com

Design Concept: The people of Whale and Star
Lead Publication Coordinator: Jillian Taylor
Copy: Gaspar González
Editor: Kevin M. F. Platt
Translators: Charles Bernstein, Clarence Brown and W. S. Merwin, Bernard Meares, Eugene Ostashevsky, Bob Perelman, Kevin M. F. Platt

Cover: (Detail) *The House: Still Whole*, 2007, Pigment print, 30 x 36 inches, by Enrique Martínez Celaya, copyright © Enrique Martínez Celaya

Distributed exclusively by University of Nebraska Press
1111 Lincoln Mall
Lincoln, Nebraska 68588-0630
www.nebraskapress.unl.edu
Tel: 800/755 1105
Fax: 800/526 2617

Library of Congress Control Number: 2008925256

ISBN: 978-0-9799752-0-2